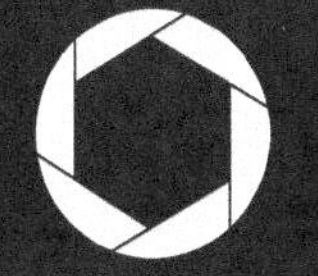

Digital Cameras in the Classroom

Mary Ploski Seamon
Eric J. Levitt

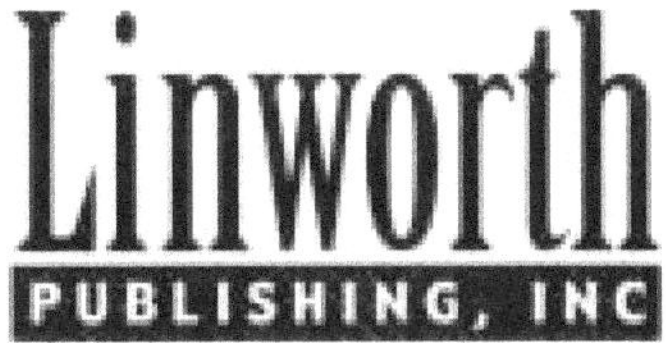

Library of Congress Cataloging-in-Publication Data

Seamon, Mary Ploski, 1943-
Digital cameras in the classroom / Mary Ploski Seamon and Eric J. Levitt.
p. cm.
Includes bibliographical references and index.
ISBN 1-58683-095-3
1. Photography in education. 2. Photography--Digital techniques--Handbooks, manuals, etc. 3. Digital cameras--Handbooks, manuals, etc. I. Levitt, Eric J., 1970- II. Title.
TR816.S43 2003
371.33'52--dc21

2003043337

Published by Linworth Publishing, Inc.
480 East Wilson Bridge Road, Suite L
Worthington, Ohio 43085

ISBN: 1-58683-095-3

5 4 3 2 1

Table of Contents

List of Figures

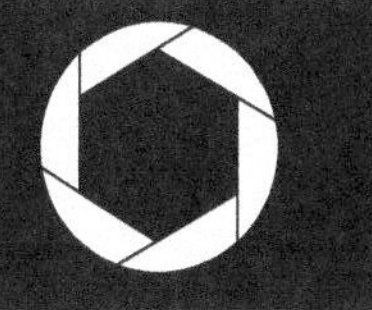

Introduction

> *"He who can no longer pause to wonder and stand rapt in awe is as good as dead; his eyes are closed."*
>
> ***—Albert Einstein***

It is mystifying. As we worked on our most recent book, *Technology Timesavers: Simple Steps to Increasing Classroom Productivity*, we discovered that there was very little information about using digital photography in the classroom. No books — few articles — we couldn't help but wonder, why not?

Digital Photography Is Powerful

Few people can ignore their first experience in using a digital camera. The idea that you can preview your film — still or moving — immediately is too good to be true. The fact that we can take pictures and send them immediately across country to family and friends is mind-boggling. The immediacy of digital photography makes it a necessary adjunct to other technology.

So why wasn't digital photography being mentioned in educational materials or outlined in technology integration plans? It seemed digital photography was a natural extension to supplement the widespread technology implementation that was taking place. There wasn't any better medium than digital imagery to use in identifying essential information when describing process steps and procedures.

Active Learning

Digital imagery seems to be a perfect way to enhance learning experiences and activities appropriate for students. After all, how better to describe who we are than through photography? We can sequence events. We can look for relationships.

Digital imagery provides a way for us to show students that history is about real people and real events. We can make school more relevant. We can build opportunities for students to make real world connections and to use varied and complex thinking.

So Why Was Digital Photography Being Ignored?

We can only speculate that digital photography was slow to move into the classroom because of the perceived fragility of the cameras or because of the perception that it wasn't affordable. Both of those reasons are inaccurate today. The cost of digital cameras has plummeted and the cameras are sturdy.

Another reason that we speculate digital photography was ignored was that it was perceived to be difficult to use the images. How do you download the images and use them in PowerPoint? How can you insert a video into a useable format?

The time to use digital cameras for standards based instruction has arrived. We hope that this book will show the way for reluctant users. We have provided numerous examples of lessons that naturally utilize digital photography.

Key Areas to Consider

Digital Cameras in the Classroom covers what we believe are the key areas:

- The instructional framework for using digital photography is key to incorporating it into the classroom. We all know that if something does not make strong instructional sense for improving student learning that it is an unnecessary frill.
- How do you select a camera? It is bewildering. We explore some of the things you should consider when selecting a camera. Do you really need a high-end camera for general classroom use? Point-and-shoot cameras are inexpensive and fulfill most requirements for general classroom use.
- So you have a camera, how can you use it? What are some of the advantages of using digital photography? This is an idea generator for thinking about how you can use digital photography in your classroom.
- New ideas and ways of looking at traditional student learning modules provide a blueprint for using digital photography in the classroom. Adding digital photography to the classroom is not adding on—it is adding to what you are currently doing.
- Getting the pictures from the camera to the computer is scary. We try to demystify this task.
- Finally, how do you use digital photography? What are some freeware programs that will simplify what you or your students can do?

Digital photography belongs in the classroom. The uses are many. The cost is affordable. Best of all—students will love it!

Chapter 1

Going Digital

> *"A picture is worth a thousand words."*
>
> ***—Confucius***

Do you remember getting your first camera? That first camera was like a rite of passage—delivered under the Christmas tree or received as a birthday present. It was a big present. You probably treated it with great care. You reveled in the power of being able to take a picture and have a permanent record of an event or a person. It was overwhelming. And it probably was stored away quickly. Who knew that film was so expensive? Who knew that it cost a fortune to develop the pictures? (Okay, admit it, parents knew all those things and more, but we ignored it.)

You took pictures anyway. Until you ran out of money and the camera was put away in the back of the closet.

Times Have Changed

That isn't the case anymore. Digital cameras make picture taking affordable. No film—no waiting to develop film—the cameras provide instant gratification. Take a picture and share it with everyone on your e-mail list. Poof, it's being viewed across the country.

Children are bombarded by visual images. Whether it's the latest action-packed game or TV show, it seems we live and breathe through images. One of the most popular syndicated shows on TV, "America's Most Wanted," has a high level of viewer involvement and viewer success in solving crimes through pictorial imagery and simulation. We would rather "see" something than interpret it through other means. During the Vietnam War and Desert Shield, coverage on TV changed our view of war. Instead of the intellectual exercise involved in reading about casualties, we saw it firsthand. We emotionally connected to the images.

I Can See Clearly Now

We are a visual society. Still and motion pictures are unlimited in their usage everywhere—everywhere it seems but in the classroom. If we wish to effectively teach the children in our classrooms, we must use a variety of instructional strategies to reach individual children. Students have an astounding array of learning styles, readiness levels, and learning profiles and we must teach them the same content. That is truer today than at any other time. The requirements of the "No Child Left Behind Act" have ensured that all children—rich or poor, black or white, English speaking or limited English speaking—have access to the same curriculum and instruction. Based on challenging state standards in reading and mathematics, No Child Left Behind requires that states implement statewide accountability systems.

In teaching content to diverse learners, effective teachers help students internalize basic concepts. Teachers understand that unless the content is connected to the "real world," the student has little chance of ever using the knowledge. If we were to teach students to play volleyball, for example, we wouldn't spend days or months having students define "spike" or in describing the size of the court or the height of the net. Instead, we would engage students actively by placing them on a volleyball court and then teach them the rules of the game as it is played. While it is true that some students may excel and have better hand and eye coordination than others, they will all be able to learn the basic rules for playing volleyball and be able to put those rules to work in a game.

Experiential learning—having students learn by doing—is superior to rote learning. While an effective teacher would never teach a sport by imparting information—all of the rules and procedures—without practicing on a court or field, we tend to teach basic content information by doing just that. It is easy to forget that basic fact when we are focusing on the subjects of language arts, math, science, or social studies.

Engaging Students

So what are we to do? How do we provide opportunities for students to do the "heavy lifting" of learning? How can an effective teacher engage students actively in learning? If the teacher is working harder than the student, isn't something wrong?

Encouraging students to engage in active learning is a five-fold process. We must:

1. relate what is being learned to what a student knows and has experienced,
2. provide time for students to reflect on what they have accomplished to deepen their understanding,
3. provide multiple examples of basic concepts so that all students have an opportunity to connect to the learning,
4. provide opportunities of students to practice what is learned, and
5. use concrete examples to help students connect to abstract ideas.

One method for doing this is through digital photography.

Concrete Learning

Digital photography has arrived. It provides a new way of learning. Digital photography enlists students with interesting and engaging tasks that link directly to the real world.

Some learners need to work with ideas and understandings at a concrete level. Digital photography — still or motion — is a wonderful way to teach basic lessons. How better to teach than through photography as we are studying:

- Story Narrative
- Compare/Contrast
- Genealogy
- The World We Live in
- Hands-on Science
- Oral Histories
- Community Issues/Problems
- Linking Past with Present
- Who Are We?

Advantages of Going Digital

There are many advantages to using digital photography. Digital photography is easy to use and makes photographs instantly accessible. We can put them on the Web, e-mail them to others, use them to illustrate a story in a word processing document, use them in PowerPoint presentations, or sequence a story with them.

While the cost of the equipment may have been a factor in the decision to use digital photography years ago, today's digital camera can cost as little as $29.00. They come in various sizes — from palm size to typical camera size. They can be tailored to the hands of young children. The cost is a small price to pay for pictures that instantly convey information that the spoken or written word does not. The human mind rapidly perceives and uses visual information.

Real World Connections

Digital photography is a way to build opportunities for students to make real world connections and to use varied and complex thinking. Whether it is making local history come alive or explaining what happens as the seasons change, digital photography can make learning more concrete and accessible.

Visual images are an important way to communicate. We learn to accept certain pictures as the way things ought to be through visual imagery. Whether it was the negative power of "Joe Camel" or other imagery, advertisers have long known that the visual image is as important — if not more important— than words alone.

Chapter 2

Selecting a Digital Camera

"He who asks a question is a fool for five minutes; he who does not ask a question is a fool forever."

—Chinese Proverb

Where Do I Begin?

When it comes to digital photography, the question, "Where do I begin?" tops the list. For any person new to digital cameras and digital photography, this may be the only question that comes to mind. Busy teachers do not always have the time to really investigate what type of digital camera would best meet their needs and the needs of their students.

Frequently, these types of purchases are left to a media specialist or a school technology coordinator. However, if you are ever in a position to purchase a digital camera for your classroom, it is helpful to know some of the basics when it comes to choosing the right one for you.

Easier said than done ... right? Sure, it can be intimidating walking through the local electronics store and seeing rows of cameras — expensive cameras — all with different features, capabilities and appearances. How do you even begin to determine which one is the right one? This chapter will take you through a step-by-step guide to figuring out the digital camera landscape. Keeping in mind that this book is probably not being read by large numbers of technophiles, but probably teachers and media specialists who are primarily interested in using this exciting medium to enhance their curriculum, technical explanations will be short, to-the-point, and written for the layperson. So, relax and sit back while we take a look at some issues to consider when selecting a digital camera.

A Pixel for Your Thoughts

The first consideration when selecting a digital camera is the number of pixels it will shoot. Pixels are tiny little squares that make up the larger picture. Think of a tiled mosaic in which each individual tile contributes to the finished work. Pixels are important because generally the more you have, the higher the quality of the picture. Often, the term resolution is used to describe the number of pixels per inch (or any unit of measurement) in a picture at a given size.

How many pixels is enough? It depends on what the final product is going to be. The low end of digital cameras are point-and-shoot cameras that usually have a pixel resolution under one million. Although these are generally the least expensive type of digital camera, be aware that you typically get what you pay for. Granted, pictures taken with a point-and-shoot digital camera will not be of photojournalistic quality, but they should more than suffice for a wide range of classroom applications such as student presentations, bulletin boards, reports, Web pages, electronic slideshows, and virtually any type of everyday use. Because they are fully automatic, point-and-shoot cameras are often a less expensive, ideal solution for the classroom environment.

Multi-megapixel cameras are the next step up from point and shoot cameras. Multi-megapixel cameras shoot images using a resolution over one million pixels. Of course, the end result is higher quality pictures that can be used in a wider range of classroom applications including more serious types of student publications or exhibits. In addition to the higher cost, multi-megapixel cameras usually offer the photographer more control over taking and adjusting the picture. Enhancements such as zoom, manual focus, automatic exposure, and various other features and effects make this type of camera more flexible in the type and variety of pictures that can be taken.

Professional Cameras

In a dream world, we would all have a professional digital camera at our disposal. However, the reality is that while they shoot at a much higher resolution (over 2 million pixels), their cost is usually prohibitive, especially to educators.

Digital Video Cameras

Some schools and teachers consider an all-in-one approach when it comes to selecting a digital camera. Today's digital video cameras (these are video cameras that actually record to digital tape) often have the capability of taking still digital photos as well. Usually, by simply switching a button from video recorder to still image, taking digital pictures is a breeze. Often digital video cameras use very small memory chips with a great deal of storage space to store digital pictures.

Another possibility when it comes to digital video cameras is pulling out pictures from individual frames shot in video footage. With special software, one can literally pull out individual frames as photos from thousands of frames in a video. Some drawbacks are the time it takes to do this as well as the fact that digital video cameras often save images in a much lower pixel resolution than digital still cameras.

Taking and Saving Pictures: How Much Storage Do I Need?

Now that you have decided how much resolution is enough resolution, the next big decision is determining the number of pictures your digital camera should store. The main factor here is determining what type of storage medium will suit your needs. Not too many years ago, the only option available to save pictures taken with a digital camera was a 3.5-inch floppy disk. It was, and still is, a great choice for storing digital images, especially in a classroom setting. While a floppy disk can store a relatively small number of pictures, the ease of use and affordability make it an attractive option.

For a class doing an outdoors science lab, the teacher can simply bring a stack of inexpensive floppy disks to use for storing pictures. Once back in the classroom, the pictures can be read directly from the floppy disk or copied to the computer and deleted from the disk. The main drawback is that floppy disks can usually only hold fewer than twenty pictures depending on the resolution setting of the camera. If a greater storage solution is what you need, take a look at the next section.

See You in a Flash

Flash memory cards have quickly become one of the most common forms of storing digital images. However, even though they are common, this does not mean that they are universal. Flash memory cards are very small chips that fit directly in the camera. For their size, they hold large quantities of photos depending on their capacity (i.e. 16 megabytes, 32 megabytes, 64 megabytes, etc.). To compare, a floppy disk can hold 1.4 megabytes of photos. A 16-megabyte flash memory card can hold roughly 11 times as many pictures as a floppy disk. However, not all flash memory cards are created equally, and there a variety to choose from including PC Cards, CompactFlash cards, SmartMedia Cards, MultiMedia Cards, and even propriety flash memory like Sony Memory Sticks.

Which one do you want in your camera? It all depends. Most cameras are designed to use one type of flash memory card over another, and usually there is not much to decide. Because the amount of storage capacity depends on how much you are willing to spend, there is not really an advantage of using one flash memory card over another.

It is more helpful to compare all type of flash memory to other categories of storage like floppy disks or even mini CD-ROM storage drives. For the most part, flash memory cards are reasonably priced, easily transported, and convenient. An important consideration when choosing how to store digital camera photos is determining how the pictures will get from the camera to your computer.

Getting Images from the Camera to Your Computer

In a perfect world, the images saved on your digital camera would simply download themselves to your computer by just sitting them next to each other and making sure the power was on (in reality, this type of file transfer is not too far away). For the time being, you must determine what type of download method makes the most sense for the type of computer you plan to use.

As discussed earlier, floppy disks offer a very easy way to transfer stored images from a digital camera to a computer. Simply remove the floppy disk from the camera, insert it into almost any computer that can read floppy disks, and open the pictures directly from the floppy disk, or download them by copying the file and pasting them into a folder on your computer. If your camera uses a flash memory card to store pictures, there are other options to consider.

Many newer cameras connect to a personal computer through a USB port. This is simply a special kind of port that allows for the high-speed transfer of files from the camera to the computer through a USB cable. The flash memory card stays in the camera when downloading images this way. One drawback is that many older computers do not possess any USB ports. However, an external USB port can be connected to your computer. It will allow you to transfer images using this method. Overall, this is a fast, convenient way to download pictures.

For cameras or computers that do not support a USB connection, images can sometimes be transferred using a flash card reader. This device connects to a computer via a USB port or a serial port (a different, but slower kind of port). After taking pictures, insert the flash memory card into the reader and follow the instructions for downloading the pictures. Again, for computers that lack USB ports, flash memory card readers cannot always be used.

Realizing that not all computers have USB ports, some flash memory card makers also sell floppy disk adapters. These devices allow you to insert the flash memory card into the adapter, which is the same size as a regular floppy disk, and insert it into the floppy disk drive on the computer. Keep in mind that not all flash memory cards are created the same and that floppy disk adapters will work with some types but not others. In general, simply following the directions of the manufacturer will ensure that you are able to successfully download images from the digital camera to the computer.

One last point to consider is other than using an ordinary floppy disk, most cameras come shipped with specific software to assist you in downloading your pictures. This could potentially place some limitation on you because the software might need to be loaded on any computer where the pictures may be downloaded.

What Else Do I Need to Consider?

Unfortunately, just like buying a car or a television, the number of options available on digital cameras far exceeds the ability to discuss each of them in depth. Viewfinder or no viewfinder, flash type, battery type, image compression, and creative controls are just some of the many features one needs to consider when selecting a digital camera. Not that these are not important, but most of these decisions will be made as a result of how much you choose to spend on a digital camera. In other words, you do not need to worry about these options unless you have specific requirements for taking pictures such as for a school yearbook. Table 2.1 on pages 11 and 12 lists important features to consider when selecting a digital camera.

Table 2.1: Selecting a Digital Camera

Type of Camera	Description
Point-and-Shoot	Simple to use straight out of the box. Lower quality pictures for a lower price. Acceptable for almost any type of classroom application.
Multi-megapixel	Also fairly easy to use, higher picture resolution means higher quality pictures. Usually higher cost includes access to more features such as automatic exposure, flash control, and LCD viewfinder.
Professional Camera	High-end camera that takes exceptional digital photos, but is cost prohibitive to most educators.
Digital Video Recorder	Camera capable of taking full motion digital videos as well as digital still images. Has capacity to store large numbers of pictures but usually at a lower resolution than even point-and-shoot cameras.
Storage Type	**Description**
Floppy Disk	Simple, inexpensive, convenient way to store digital photos. Major restriction is a relatively small storage capacity.
Flash Memory Card	Small, fairly inexpensive chips that possess storage capacity up to hundreds of times that of floppy disks. Several different styles of flash memory mean several different types of readers and software may be necessary. Limits downloading pictures to computers that can read the card.
Mini-CD	Fairly expensive medium to store hundreds or thousands of pictures. Mini-CDs usually require an adapter to make them readable in standard CD-ROM drives. Because of the sensitivity of the CD burner in the camera, not a great choice for everyday classroom use.
Transferring (Downloading) Images	**Description**
Floppy Disk Transfer	Easy, quick way to download images to virtually any computer that can read floppy disks.
USB Port	Port type found on newer computers and computers that have external USB hubs allowing multiple connections. Very fast and probably will become the industry standard.
Serial Cable	Older, but more common technology found on older computers. Easy to connect but much slower downloading images.
Parallel Port	Not widely seen in today's newer digital cameras. Connects camera through parallel port that is often occupied by a printer. Besides being slow, parallel port connections are not widely used.
Firewire Card	Firewire is a relatively new technology designed by Apple Computers that allows extremely fast transfer of digital images. Requires a Firewire card as well as appropriate cable.
Flash Memory Card Reader	Reader that usually connects to a computer through a USB port. Enables you to insert a flash memory card into the reader and then download the images to a computer. Not all readers read all flash memory cards.
Flash Memory Card Floppy Disk Adapter	For computers that are unable to connect flash memory card readers, floppy disk adapters can be used. However, not all floppy disk adapters work with all flash memory cards.

Table 2.1: Selecting a Digital Camera (continued)

Extras	**Description**
Automatic	Speed and shutter settings automatically controlled by the camera.
Manual	For more adept photographers, manual control offers greater flexibility and freedom in taking pictures.
Zoom	Enables camera to get in close on a shot from far away.
Flash	Automatic vs. manual offers different degrees of artistic control.
Batteries	**Description**
Alkaline Batteries	Inexpensive way to keep camera running, but short life means frequent replacements.
Battery Charger	Most common way to charge camera batteries while not in use.
AC Adapter	Enables picture taking even when batteries are recharging.

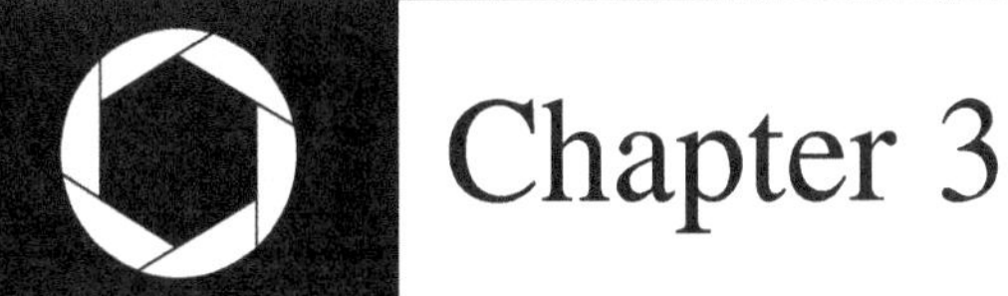

Photography Basics

> *"Practice is everything."*
>
> ***—Periander***

Schools are busy places. Students and teachers are often in constant motion. Most of us are in "rush" mode at school, and we do not always consider some of the basic tenets of taking good pictures ... composition, lighting, and framing to name a few. Taking pictures of various classroom activities means being ready for that "must have" shot. It also means that things like the flash and exposure better be right to avoid missing that golden opportunity when a student makes a spectacular discovery, or when students on a nature hike encounter an interesting plant or animal. Taking pictures with students actively engaged in learning, forces us to look at how we frame shots. If you have not noticed, photos of students and student work generally fall into two categories: photographs that clearly and vibrantly depict the subject, or photos in which the subject gets lost or overwhelmed depending on basic considerations like their placement in the viewfinder before clicking the shutter. We know what you are saying, "I just wanted to point and click without having to worry about stuff like this."

Do not despair. These tips are not essential in the operation of your digital camera, but they sure help with the learning curve when it comes to taking interesting and exciting pictures. This chapter will walk you through some of the most handy photography basics and they will help you to begin taking the best quality pictures as quickly as possible.

Be a Composer

Our aim is to show how these basics can be applied by teachers and students during their daily lives. The first area to consider on your road to taking better pictures is *composition*. Think about how you write a paper or essay. It is not something that you just throw together without careful thought and consideration.

Taking good pictures requires some attention to the details, even if your desire is to point and click your way to digital camera nirvana. At the risk of stating the obvious, always have your camera ready for taking a shot. This sounds so incredibly simple, but it is not always the case.

At school, opportunities to take digital photos pop-up constantly; but taking the pictures is only possible if the camera is charged, accessible, and equipped. There are few moments quite as disappointing as when you finally get up the nerve to check-out the school's digital camera only to find out the power was out the night before and the camera battery did not charge. It is always a good idea to have at least one back-up battery that remains fully charged.

Before any composition can take place, the camera must be accessible to you and other faculty. Treating digital cameras like the crown jewels and locking them up in the vault or other nether regions of the school restricts the teachers' access to them. While I do not think digital cameras should be left out in the open, they should remain reasonably accessible to any teacher who wants to use one or wants his class to use one.

Once the camera is checked-out, make sure that it is equipped with whatever you need. If you are going on a three-day field trip, and it is a camera that uses 3.5-inch floppy disks, bring plenty along with you. Other considerations include camera bags, telephoto lenses, and tripods.

Be Still My Heart

The next step to taking better pictures is to *be still* when taking the shot. Considering that you might be shooting a whirlwind student activity at some point, being still is critical to avoiding blurry shots. This is particularly hard to do when the subject is in constant motion.

Some basic things to consider are holding the camera with two hands to stabilize it or maybe getting a tripod stand to remove any movement. A tripod is particularly useful for younger children who may not be able to hold a camera still. Tripods are available for under $20. Particularly useful are the ultralight tripods that are now available. One of which is the UltraPod. To find out more about the UltraPod, visit <http://www.pedcopods.com/products.htm>.

Use the Viewfinder

In the real-world school use of digital cameras, many pictures will need to be shot quickly and sometimes with little notice. One relatively easy tip to follow is to use the viewfinder rather than the LCD display (if the camera has one).

An example that comes to mind is a recent state conference in which several teachers from our school district received various awards. During the awards presentation, we were asked to take some shots of them for posterity. When looking through the LCD display, it was difficult to see the teachers (the lights were quite dim), and the image was jumping all over the place. Imagine trying to look at the LCD display as several teachers walked up to the podium. Additionally, holding the camera about a foot away to look at the LCD display made the camera less stable for shooting a picture. The best option was to turn off the LCD display and use the trusty viewfinder which allowed a clearer view of the subjects. It also helped to remove the jitter associated with using the LCD display.

To Pose or Not to Pose

Most professionals say don't do it. Posed shots are great for individual yearbook photos, but in most other instances they are perceived as contrived and boring. Taking a photo of a subject who is acting naturally usually produces much more favorable results. For example, scan through your school newspaper or yearbook and look at the posed photos for athletics or any club or organization. Now, look at any candid, unposed shots of any of the above and note the differences. The unposed shots are almost certainly going to generate a greater sense of excitement, animation, and enthusiasm.

Where Do You Want Me?

We have all heard or asked this question when getting ready to photograph someone. It is unlikely that you would respond "in the bottom-left, bottom-right, top-left, or top-right of the viewfinder," but somewhere in one of those four locations is where the focal point of the picture should be. Placing the subject near one of the corners, but not completely in one of the corners is called the *rule of thirds.* Take a look at Figure 3.1. Imagine the subject of your shot split into thirds and try to position the subject in one of the areas intersected by two lines.

Figure 3.1: The Rule of Thirds

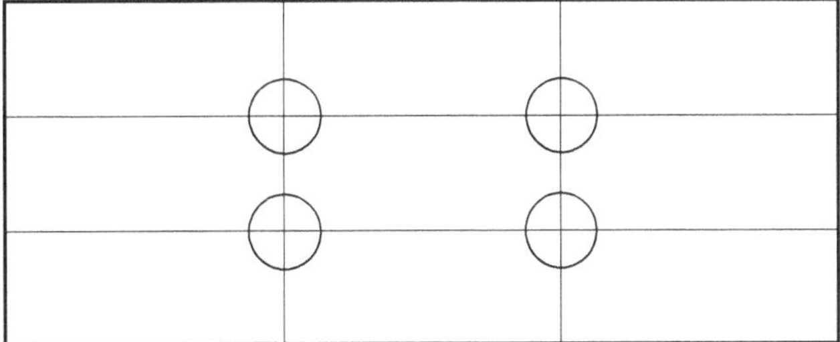

Consider outdoor projects in which the landscape or environment plays an important role in the unit of study. Taking pictures of students aligned smack-dab in the middle of the picture lessens the impact of the natural surroundings. A sporting event is another scenario where the space around the subject can tell as much about the action being photographed as the subject itself.

Don't Skimp on the Resolution

Another composition tip is to shoot at the highest resolution available on your camera. In the early days of digital photography when floppy disks were the main storage medium, this was a serious concern because higher resolution meant that fewer pictures could be stored on a disk. This could mean the difference between saving ten high-resolution pictures versus eighteen to twenty lower resolution shots. The same holds true today except that using compact flash memory cards means maybe only being able to store one-hundred pictures on a 32 megabyte card at the highest resolution setting versus 150 pictures at a lower setting.

Fortunately, memory cards are available in much larger sizes (64 mb, 96 mb, etc.); couple this advantage with a memory card's portability and easy accessibility, and worrying about file size should not be an issue because of memory limitations. In schools, high resolution shots are usually desirable because so much of what is photographed at school gets printed out in some form or fashion whether for a research paper, newsletter, or brochure. Even if you are planning to post pictures to your school's Web site, it is easy to scale down the size of a digital image in a program like PhotoShop. However, increasing the resolution of photos is not as easy and the results are usually not as good as one might hope.

Light Your Way

Some of the best and worst pictures taken at school or school events are tied very closely to the lighting. Often, different times of the day offer better lighting than others, such as in the early morning and late afternoon. Unfortunately for school people, these are the times when we are probably least likely to be shooting student activities or events. In fact, most digital photography takes place indoors in sometimes poorly lit areas of a building. This is why it is imperative to not only use, but to understand how the flash on your particular camera operates most effectively. Maybe it is the fluorescent lighting or windowless areas of the school, but an awful lot of pictures taken indoors at school have an unattractive yellow-green tint to them. Some of this could be remedied by using the flash when appropriate. So, read your manual. However, look closely at the picture you are planning to take. Ask yourself, "Is it possible to take this picture elsewhere or at a different time to allow for more natural light to illuminate the subject?" This might not be the case, but consider it to reduce the number of *yellow-greenies* you take.

A Good Frame Can Save a Bad Picture

It is not always true, but effectively framing the subject of a photograph can mean the difference between a so-so photo or one that is a knockout. The subject of your photograph should be just that… the subject. Too often, pictures of classroom activities and students are group shots taken from a distance to get everyone in the picture. The end result is a far-off picture of a crowd of people that lacks dynamic flair and is usually unexciting. Another less than optimal result occurs when taking pictures of some classroom activity. Often, the photographer will take a shot of the entire classroom to make sure to include everybody. Egalitarian, yes, but visually stimulating, no. When framing a shot, try to focus closely on the subject. Some refer to this as a "tight shot" in which extraneous detail is logically left out of the frame. Now of course there will be those shots when the subject is standing next to some cute sign at an exotic locale, where moving further away from the subject is acceptable to prove that the person actually visited the largest ball of twine in the U.S. However, other photos, especially school photos, carry more "oomph" and deliver greater impact when the subject can be seen clearly. The bottom line is that people want to see faces, and that means getting up-close to your subject to shoot. Would you rather have one great shot of one student or a lousy shot of 30 students?

Learning How

For those teachers and students who would like to do further research, the following Web sites provide good information.

The Kodak Digital Picture Center, <http://www.kodak.com/US/en/home/dpc.shtml>, provides a plethora of resources. Among the topics are the following:

- how to get a quality print from a digital picture,
- how to e-mail your pictures,
- the 5 top reasons to go digital,
- how to explore the digital learning center, and
- frequently asked questions.

Learning to Take Digital Pictures, <http://www.sipixdigital.com/pdf/ebook.pdf>, is a great site. The site provides ten tips for taking better pictures.

Digital Photography, An Online Course, <http://www.photocourse.com/>, provides technical information for advanced students.

Say Cheese, <http://www.saycheese.com/>, provides information for the beginning student on composition and camera selection.

Digital Photography with Windows XP, <http://www.microsoft.com/windowsxp/digitalphotography/>, provides a variety of informational sites ranging from getting pictures from your camera to your computer to tips for photo composition.

The Internet Brothers: Digital Photography, <http://internetbrothers.com/phototips.htm>, provides information on digital techniques and digital storage techniques.

HP's Digital Imaging, <http://www.homeandoffice.hp.com/hho/us/eng/digital_photography.html>, provides numerous articles on how to take pictures, selecting a camera, and looks particularly at backyard photography and family photography.

Chapter 4

Picture This

> *"There are two kinds of teachers: the kind that fill you with so much quail shot that you can't move, and the kind that just gives you a little prod behind and you jump to the skies."*
>
> ***—Robert Frost***

"So are we going to do anything in class today?" How often do we cringe when we hear that question or its accompaniment, *"Did I miss anything in class yesterday?"*

We would like to think that classes are filled with important stuff—stuff that children must know and be able to do in order to function in this complex world. But, our more cynical students easily dismiss what we may consider to be important information. Unless students are engaged and are able to connect to what is being taught, it is dismissed as "nothing." Our students dismiss lectures, drill and practice, and worksheets that emphasize memorization of facts and procedures—activities that create a heavy burden of preparation for teachers—quickly.

In teacher preparation classes we learned how to teach math, or how to teach social studies, or how to teach English or just plain, how to *teach*. We assumed that students would come into the classroom (*on time*), sit down (*quietly*), and absorb everything that we had learned and wished to share about the subject. Somehow we didn't think that the textbook might be boring and disconnected from the lives of our students. The current emphasis on standards based learning is further exacerbating this problem.

Standards Based Learning

With the emphasis on academic standards, the tendency in the classroom is to narrow the curriculum. We feel a pressing need to address all the standards methodically—after all, students will be assessed on what they know and understand about those standards. However, it is only through cross-curricular or interdisciplinary projects that we are truly able to encourage students to become active participants in their own learning.

Academic narrowing of curriculum occurs in many classrooms because teachers believe that a passive instructional approach is necessary. Test developers and textbook companies claim that they have developed a foolproof program to teach standards. Educators may acquiesce to that line of thinking because they have not had the necessary professional development to question that assertion.

Teaching the Essential Skills

To demystify standards based instruction, we need to know what it is. Standards provide outlines to students, parents, and teachers what will be learned at each grade level or in each course. Accordingly, standards based curriculum is a set of instructional materials and teaching practices that enable all students the access and opportunity to know the essential knowledge and be able to accomplish the skills identified by the academic standards.

If we are to teach strong standards based curriculum, our responsibility is to:

1. provide relevant learning opportunities that are active and connected to the world outside the classroom,
2. promote life long learning for all students through high expectations for learning,
3. support instructional methods that engage students in learning that is developmentally appropriate, and
4. allow the teacher to be a facilitator by engaging students in questioning, thinking, problem solving, and reflecting on their learning.

As educators, we have a pivotal role in creating learning opportunities in which more students than ever before achieve the academic proficiencies that they will need in the future. We can do this by connecting instruction to the lives of students.

Using an Interactive Approach

Students do not become engaged in what they are studying unless we use an interactive approach that encourages involvement through inquiry-based, hands-on activities. A classroom emphasis on facts and rote memorization ensures that students remember the information until they are tested. After the test, the information is erased from memory if it isn't connected to what the student already knows. If we want students to build knowledge, we must do it through projects that connect the student to the larger world. It is this learning that students carry with them. An engaging curriculum gets kids to think deeply, care about their world, and helps them see their place within that world.

Engaging Students Through Digital Imagery

One way of engaging students is through digital imagery. It has been said that perception is reality. We all see things differently. One of the important tasks of the teachers is to encourage students to express their unique perspective of the subject being taught. It is through this manipulation of ideas and objects that we become responsible for our learning. Becoming literate involves our ability to use a variety of information resources to synthesize, create, and communicate meaning. Classroom projects are a great way to make this happen.

Digital imagery with its immediacy and its magical power—a moment in time captured forever—engages students. The power of being able to document experiences or to use photography for projects and slide shows intrigues students. Digital photography is experiential. Students become involved with experience.

Experiential learning encourages greater student involvement in the curriculum. By using our community and the natural connection to the school community, we ensure that students will have numerous opportunities to reflect, problem-solve, and collaborate with others. It is through this engagement of dealing with what is happening in the world and connecting students to their place in that world that we make the curriculum sing.

Digital cameras, which are becoming more affordable every day, can be readily available in the classroom. Ideally, a teacher would have three to five cameras available for student use. With multiple storage devices accessible, students may have their own floppy disk, CD-ROM, or other device to save their pictures. For most classroom projects, a low-resolution camera is sufficient.

Teaching students to use the cameras can be done quickly and easily. Even if you do not have expertise with digital cameras, a media specialist, a parent, or an older student would probably be able to provide a one-day photography workshop for you and your students.

Photography Workshop

The photography workshop provides an opportunity for students and teachers to learn three essential skills:

1. how to take pictures,
2. how to move pictures from the camera to the computer, and
3. how to use the images in a word processing document, on a Web page, or in a PowerPoint presentation.

The workshop is also an opportunity for the teacher or media specialist to encourage students to be respectful of the equipment. That should not be that great a problem. Most students, even very young primary students, have already learned to be careful with valued possessions.

Family Involvement

Parental involvement is critical to a student's academic success, and enlisting the help of parents as the students learn to use digital cameras is a wonderful idea. These activities are family-friendly. Most parents will feel comfortable assisting the student at home if they are given an overview of the lessons expected.

So What Can I Teach?

The next chapter explores lessons that incorporate digital cameras and standards based instruction.

Chapter 5

Seeing Is Believing

"The mediocre teacher tells. The good teacher explains. The superior teacher demonstrates. The great teacher inspires."

—William A. Ward

Into what kind of lessons can digital photography be incorporated? Most any kind of lesson will work. This chapter provides some suggestions for topics. In the first series of lesson plans, we provide a one-sheet overview of key elements to include in the lesson plan:

- Overview
- Standards
- Objective
- Digital Camera Use
- Lesson
- Products
- Assessment

In several cases, we have taken the one-page summaries and given a sample student project. These are meant to be idea generators.

Letter Talk/Number Talk

Primary Classroom

Overview:

Students will take pictures of common classroom objects. Students will help each other identify the beginning letter of the object or students will take pictures that illustrate numbers — i.e., one desk, two people, three crayons, etc.

Standards:

- The student will begin using oral language, pictures, or letters to create stories about experiences, people, objects, and events.
- The student will begin following one- and two-step oral directions.
- The student will begin identifying pictures as sources of information.
- The student will begin organizing information on the basis of observation.
- The student will demonstrate the ability to use pictures, oral language, or letters to create stories about experiences, people, objects, and events.

Objective:

Students will develop a new understanding as they connect familiar information to new information.

Lesson:

1. Teacher will review opening letters and numbers.
2. Using manipulatives and common classroom objects, teacher will lead students in saying words and counting.
3. Teacher will assign cooperative groups to take pictures of common classroom objects. The cooperative groups will be divided as follows:
   a. One student will describe the pictures taken.
   b. One student will be the photographer.
   c. One student will direct the photographer to take pictures of objects that she/he discovers.

Products:

Students will create their own alphabet books or number books.

Assessment:

Students will share what they know about letters and sounds with a small group of their peers.

Who Am I?

Grades 2–5

Overview:

Students will take digital photographs that illustrate who they are. Each student will create a storyboard that helps them see themselves and their story more clearly. After mapping out their storyboard, each student will take a digital camera home to take pictures.

Standards:

- The student will demonstrate the ability to identify pictures, charts, tables of contents, and diagrams as sources of information.
- The student will continue gathering information from a variety of sources, including those accessed through the use of technology.

Objective:

Students will use a digital camera to describe who they are and what's important to them. Students will tell stories about their family and themselves.

Digital Camera Use:

Students will take pictures of family members, hobbies, or objects that are important to them.

Lesson:

1. Students will read biographies at the appropriate developmental level. (They may also read autobiographies that other students have written to use as a model for their own writing.)
2. Each student will complete a storyboard that illustrates the important events and people in their life.
3. Students will use a digital camera to take pictures that are representative of the events in the storyboard.
4. Students will write their own autobiography and illustrate it with the digital pictures.

Products:

1. Students will write a story about themselves and illustrate the story with pictures they have taken.
2. They will present their story to their classmates in a PowerPoint presentation.
3. Students may research the Web for facts, lists, and illustrations that demonstrate their interests.

Assessment:

Rubrics will be developed to assess the storyboard, pictures, and autobiography.

Who Are You?

Overview:

Studying biographies can be captivating for students. Extracting information from different sources is essential to the learning process. This lesson illustrates an information-gathering process for students as they seek information by listening to and looking at resources.

Standards:

- The student will demonstrate the ability to use **literary models** to develop and refine his or her own writing style.
- The student will demonstrate the ability to gather information from a variety of sources, including those accessed through the use of technology.

Objective:

Students will gather information from various sources, organize it, and complete a biography.

Digital Camera Use:

Students will use the digital camera to capture images of a person they select. They may use the camera to illustrate hobbies and places that the person enjoys.

Lesson:

1. Students will read biographies of famous people.
2. Students will select a person they admire (younger students should select a family member or person they know).
3. Students will use Inspiration to brainstorm ideas about the characteristics they most admire in a person.
4. Students will take pictures that illustrate the characteristics of the person they admire most.

Products:

Students will write a biography and illustrate it with pictures.

Assessment:

Rubrics will be developed to assess information gathering and the writing of the biography.

Families and Communities

Overview:

A neighborhood is a place where people live, work, and play. As children grow, they begin to understanding that there is a whole world around them. Students will explore local history and develop a new perspective and a better understanding of their town. The exercise will provide students with an opportunity to understand nontraditional research methods and exercise planning and organizational skills. Initially, teams of students will chose various aspects of their community — geographical, historical, cultural, or political — to research. This pictorial study will make local history come alive by capturing the sights and sounds of the towns and cities in which they live.

Standards:

English/Language Arts

- The student will access and use information from a variety of appropriately selected sources to extend his or her knowledge.
- This unit covers standards in reading, writing, speaking, listening, and technology.

Social Studies

The student will demonstrate an understanding of the way individuals, families, and communities live and work together now and in the past. The student should be able to:

- state how personal changes are affected by the influence of peer groups and
- identify historical resources in the local community.

Objective:

Students will create a pictorial history of their community that reflects what they believe to be the seven most important sights in the community

Digital Camera Use:

Students will take digital pictures of their community and their families.

Products:

Students will create a pictorial history of their community and display it for members of the community at the local bank.

Assessment:

A rubric will be used to evaluate the information sources, selection, text, and photography in the pictorial history.

How Do You...?

Overview:

This lesson illustrates how details and sequence of directions are important in accurately describing how to do something. Students will write a 1–2 paragraph paper explaining how to make a peanut butter and jelly sandwich or other assignments that have process steps. After students write the paragraphs, they will share them with a peer who will follow the directions and attempt to accomplish the task. The classmate must be able to follow the directions and accurately create the product. Emphasis should be on the logical sequence of ideas. This activity may be used for a host of different activities including coloring Easter eggs, cutting out pumpkins, tying shoes, cutting out paper dolls, and making and flying a paper airplane.

Standards:

- The student will demonstrate the ability to follow a logical sequence of written directions to complete a task.
- The student will demonstrate the ability to use graphic representations such as charts, graphs, pictures, and graphic organizers as information sources and as a means of organizing information and events logically.
- The student will demonstrate the ability to **revise** writing for clarity, sentence variety, precise vocabulary, and effective phrasing through **collaboration**, **conferencing**, and **self-evaluation**.

Objective:

Students will learn to use more detail in their writing. Students will write a clear and concise "how to" paper. Directions will be logical and sequential. (Younger students will use pictures to begin to learn how sequence is important.)

Lesson:

1. Students should give examples of other sets of directions that must be clear.
2. Students must develop step-by-step procedures for making a peanut butter and jelly sandwich.
3. Directions should be clear and specific.
4. Students should be advised to include all steps. A classmate must be able to follow the directions in order to make a peanut butter and jelly sandwich.
5. Students will use a digital camera to sequence the activity.

Products:

Students will complete a "how to" paragraph paper explaining how to make a peanut butter and jelly sandwich.

The successful completion of the paper should supply directions for a classmate to follow in order to make a peanut butter and jelly sandwich.

Assessment:

A classmate must be able to follow all steps to successful completion. The paper will be rewritten until the classmate is successful.

The writer and the classmate will reflect on the activity and describe what made the activity successful and the barriers that slowed the completion of the task.

Sample "How To" Paper: Making a Peanut Butter and Jelly Sandwich

(With younger students, the teacher may have students place the pictures in proper sequence)

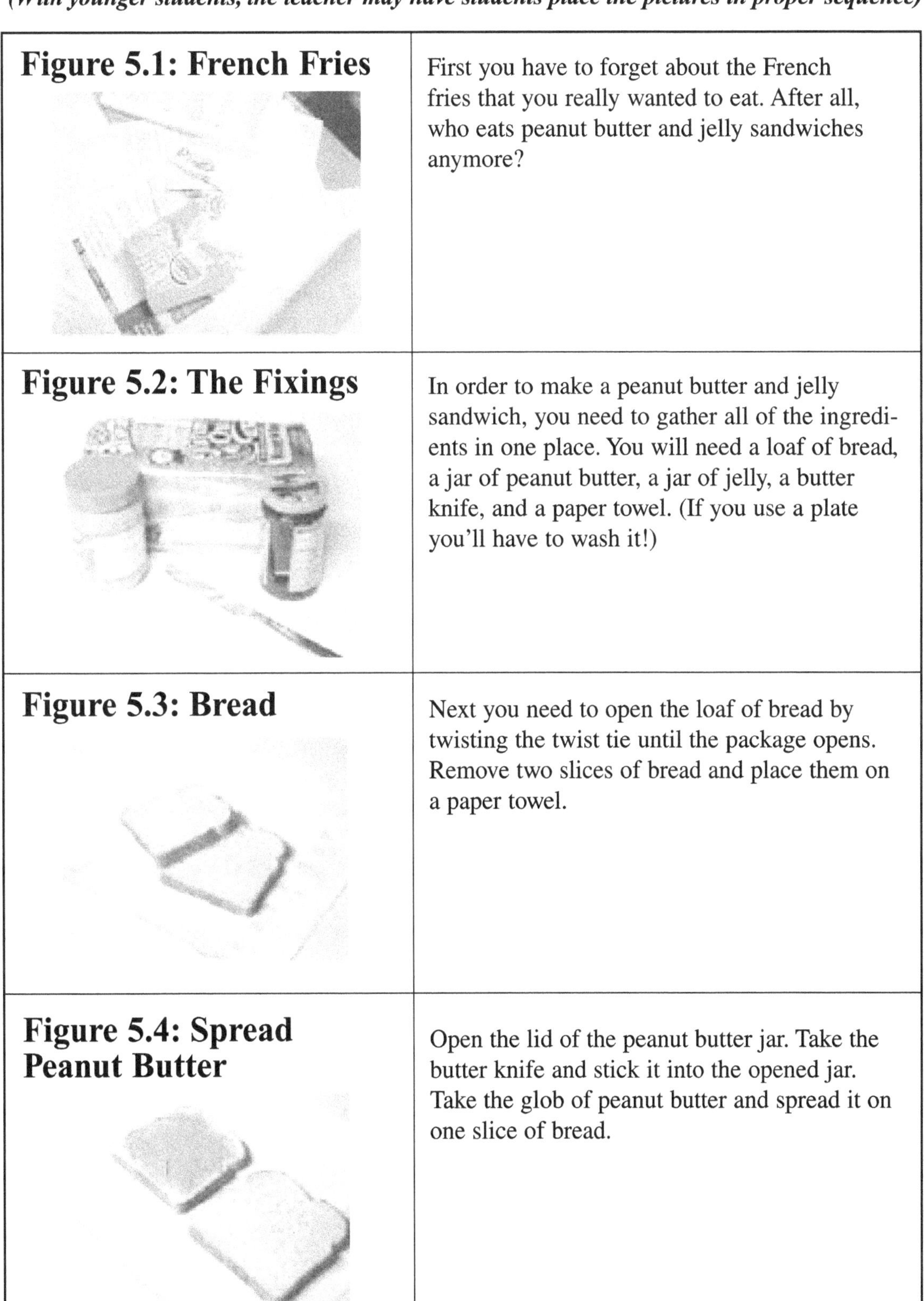

Figure 5.1: French Fries	First you have to forget about the French fries that you really wanted to eat. After all, who eats peanut butter and jelly sandwiches anymore?
Figure 5.2: The Fixings	In order to make a peanut butter and jelly sandwich, you need to gather all of the ingredients in one place. You will need a loaf of bread, a jar of peanut butter, a jar of jelly, a butter knife, and a paper towel. (If you use a plate you'll have to wash it!)
Figure 5.3: Bread	Next you need to open the loaf of bread by twisting the twist tie until the package opens. Remove two slices of bread and place them on a paper towel.
Figure 5.4: Spread Peanut Butter	Open the lid of the peanut butter jar. Take the butter knife and stick it into the opened jar. Take the glob of peanut butter and spread it on one slice of bread.

Sample "How-To" Paper (continued)

Figure 5.5: Spread Jelly 	Open the lid of the jelly jar. Take another butter knife (I know I forgot it in the picture but I really hate to use a peanut butter knife in jelly). Stick the knife in the open jelly jar. Take the glob of jelly and spread it on one slice of bread (make sure you don't mix the peanut butter with the jelly on one slice of bread).
Figure 5.6: The Finished Sandwich 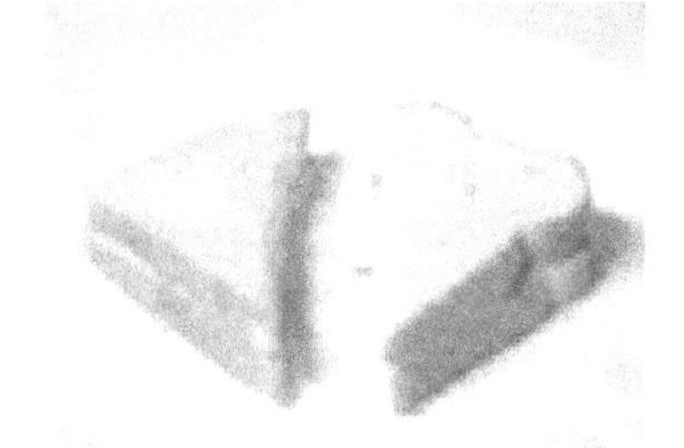	Pick up the slice of bread with peanut butter on it. Carefully put the peanut butter side of the bread on top of the jelly side of the bread. Cut the bread lengthwise to create a picture perfect peanut butter and jelly sandwich. (Now can I eat those fries?)

A Virtual Field Trip

Overview:

Students will document a field trip and create a virtual field trip for other students who have not had the opportunity to visit the site. Students will collect information about the site from personal experience and from the Web if applicable. They will research print sources to gather additional information. All information will be organized into a Web site or PowerPoint presentation.

Standards:

- The student will demonstrate the ability to use writing to explain and inform.
- The student will demonstrate the ability to use writing to learn, entertain, and describe.
- The student will demonstrate the ability to gather and organize information from a variety of sources, including those accessed through the use of technology.
- The student will demonstrate the ability to make connections between material from nonprint sources and his or her prior knowledge, other sources, and the world.

Objective:

The student will access and use information from a variety of appropriately selected sources to extend his or her knowledge.

Digital Camera Use:

Students will use digital cameras to document the field trip.

Lesson:

1. Students will use print and technology sources to investigate the area that they are going to visit.
2. Students will check out digital cameras to record significant events on the field trip.
3. Students will maintain a field trip journal to describe events that will help put pictures and other documents into perspective.
4. In cooperative learning groups, students will discuss what they saw and what pictures are most representative of the field trip.
5. Students will order information and determine the logical sequence for presenting the information to their peers.
6. Students will write text, insert pictures, and present the information to peers.

Assessment:

A rubric will be given to students and it will be used to evaluate the information collected. A rubric will be given to students and it will be used to evaluate the presentation.

Sample Virtual Field Trip: Let's Go to Camp!

Created by Pam Cook, Robin Breitenbach, Paul Brown, Teresa Cochran, Leslie Lybrand, and Kitty Smith, Cowpens Middle School, Cowpens, SC

Overview:

Although this example focuses on a field trip that students would take to Camp Sea Gull, this template could be used to describe other activities as well.

This activity was designed to familiarize sixth grade students at Cowpens Middle School in Spartanburg School District Three, Spartanburg, South Carolina with a week-long field trip they will take to Camp Sea Gull in Arapahoe, North Carolina. It is our hope that students, parents, and community members visit this site to gather background information on this exciting experience.

Standards:

- The student will demonstrate the ability to generate drafts that use a logical progression of ideas to develop a topic for a specific audience and purpose.
- The student will demonstrate the ability to develop an extended response around a central idea, using relevant supporting details.
- The student will demonstrate the ability to write multiple-paragraph compositions, friendly letters, and expressive and informational pieces.
- The student will demonstrate the ability to conduct independent research using available resources, including technology.
- The student will demonstrate the ability to summarize the information that he or she has gathered.
- The student will demonstrate the ability to present his or her research findings in a variety of formats.

Introduction:

Imagine traveling far from home. You're all packed and you meet your friends in the parking lot. Your luggage and gear are tossed into the belly of a monstrous bus. You board, and along with your teachers, you settle into comfortable seats and anticipate the journey ahead. Waving goodbye to your family, the bus lurches forward and you're off! Camp Sea Gull here we come!

Sample Virtual Field Trip (continued)

This is what our camp looks like:

Figure 5.7: The Shoreline

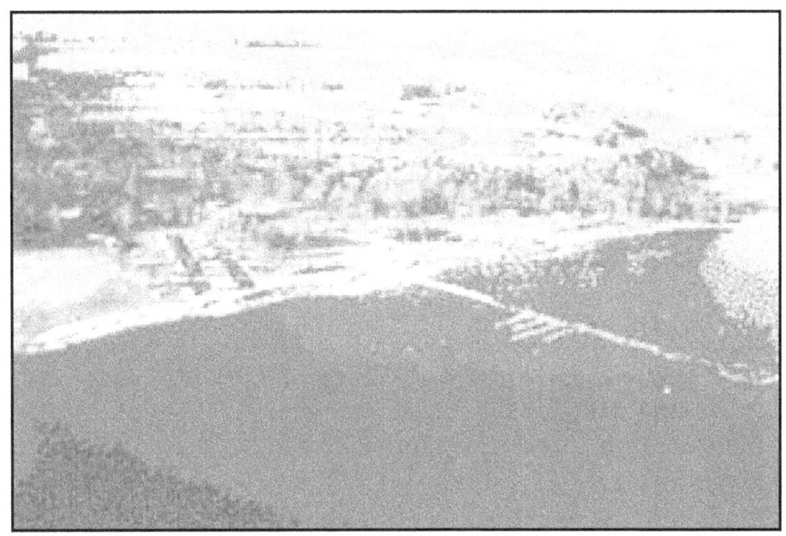

Figure 5.8: The Pier

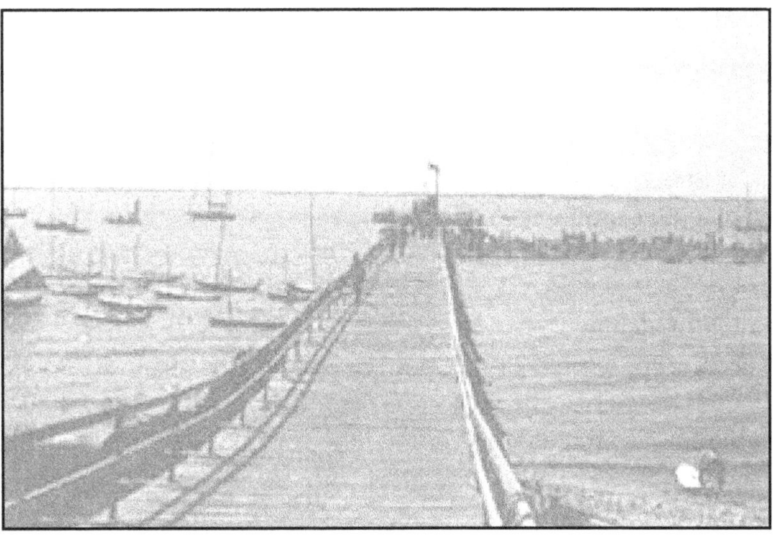

Sample Virtual Field Trip (continued)

Objectives:

- Use the Internet to gather information.
- On a map, locate Camp Sea Gull in Arapahoe, North Carolina
- Estimate the distance from Cowpens, South Carolina to Camp Sea Gull.
- View pictures of camp activities.
- Read a biographical sketch of Rachel Carson and answer questions.
- Read a recent news article about the discovery of Blackbeard's ship, the *Queen Anne's Revenge*. Explain its significance to our trip.
- Write a reflective piece of what you think your Camp Sea Gull experience will be like.
- Write a brochure, with pictures, that describes your experience to your parents.

Student Activities:

Internet Access/Map Skills

Your assignment is to access a map for North and South Carolina, download it, and print a copy for your folder.

To do this, follow the instructions below:

- Print a copy of this page so you will have a hard copy of these instructions.
- Navigate to the following Web site by placing the cursor on the Web site until a hand appears, and then double click the mouse's left button. <http://maps.yahoo.com/yahoo/yt.hm?FAM=yahoo&CMD=FILL&SEC=startdd>

Follow the instructions on the Web page using these two addresses:

Origin
150 Foster Street
Cowpens, South Carolina 29330

Destination
218 Sea Gull Landing
Arapahoe, North Carolina 28510

Answer the following questions. You will be able to get your answers from this Web site.

1. What direction will we be heading when we turn left on Hwy 70?
2. How many miles will we travel on Interstate 85?
3. When we enter camp, we will be turning off what highway?
4. How many driving hours will this trip take?

Sample Virtual Field Trip (continued)

Exploring Rachel Carson's Nature Preserve

Students are to access the Rachel Carson Web site, read the article about Rachel Carson, and answer the following questions. <http://onlineethics.org/moral/carson/main.html>

1. Who inspired Rachel Carson's interest in nature?
2. What is the title of Rachel Carson's first book?
3. Her book, *Silent Spring*, dealt with the problems of the use of pesticides and their effects on the environment. Why do you think the use of pesticides can be dangerous?

The Coast's Most Famous Pirate: Blackbeard

Students are to access the following site and answer the five "W" questions (WHO?, WHAT?, WHERE?, WHEN?, and WHY?) after reading the article.
<http://www.ocracoke-nc.com/blackbeard/treasure/95cert.htm>

Personal Response:

Students are to write a paragraph describing what they think their Camp Sea Gull experience will be like. Upon returning from camp, students will compare, in writing, their actual experience to their anticipated one.

At the camp, students will use their digital cameras and personal journals to record what they believe is the most significant experience that they had at Camp Sea Gull. Prepare a brochure for next year's class to tell them what to expect.

Let's Investigate

Overview:

In this exercise, students investigate a topic in greater depth. The lesson is ideal for connecting English/language arts and science. Students determine which details are most important. This would be excellent for science fair projects and other scientific investigation.

Standards:

Science

- Predict the results of actions based on patterns in data and experiences.
- Pose questions and problems to be investigated.
- Obtain scientific information from a variety of sources, such as Internet, electronic encyclopedias, journals, community resources, etc.

English/Language Arts

- Demonstrate the ability to generate drafts that use a logical progression of ideas to develop a topic for a specific **audience** or **purpose**.
- Demonstrate the ability to develop an extended response around a **central idea** using relevant supporting details.

Objective:

The student will use appropriate tools and techniques to gather, analyze, and interpret data.

Lesson:

1. Students will pose a problem and investigate it.
2. Students will identify issues in the natural world where steps and sequence of events are essential and explain why they are so important.
3. Students will document the problem.
4. Students will propose a solution.

Assessment:

The completed product will be evaluated according to a rubric.

Sample Investigation: Recycling

Overview:

Are you concerned about recycling? Do you think it's an important issue for our community and our state?

Standards:

Demonstrate the ability to generate drafts that use a logical progression of ideas to develop a topic for a specific audience and purpose.

Introduction:

Would you like to participate in a simulated activity involving recycling? Follow the links below to sites that will allow you the opportunity to explore the issues of recycling.

As you read, think about your neighborhood and our community as you consider the following:

- Do we have a problem with trash in our community?
- Is anyone in our community addressing the issue?
- Can we do something about the need for recycling?

Visit the following recycling site and answer the questions:

<http://www.learner.org/exhibits/garbage/intro.html>

1. How many pounds of solid trash does the average American generate?
2. What are sustainable practices?
3. What are unsustainable practices?

Click on the Solid Waste sidebar and answer the following questions:

4. Why will half of today's landfills close by the year 2003?
5. Can we burn trash? Explain your answer.

To participate in an interactive activity, click on the following sites:

<http://www.ringleader.com/quest/welcome.html>
<http://www.epa.gov/kids/>

Step 1: Visit the following recycling site and answer the questions:

Click on <http://www.epa.gov/kids/recyclecity.htm> and play the game entitled Dumptown — Recycle City

1. Name one way that Shaq's Garage helps protect our Earth.
2. What does Maria's Market give their customers for bringing back paper or plastic bags to be reused for bagging groceries?
3. How does recycling bottles and cans help the Earth?
4. Name four kinds of "hazardous waste" described by Harlin Hazzard.

Sample Investigation: Recycling (continued)

Step 2: Take Action!

Think and reflect on the following two questions:

1. What can you do to protect the environment in your town?
2. Who are the people in your town who have the influence or the power to improve the environment?

In cooperative learning groups:

1. Discuss areas of the city where trash and environmental problems are more pronounced than in other areas. Do these areas have in anything in common?
2. Are the environmental concerns in certain areas of the town?
3. Is it an isolated problem?

Step 3: Document the Problem

1. Check out the digital camera(s) from your teacher.
2. Take pictures of areas of the town that are environmentally attractive.
3. Take pictures of areas of the town that you have identified as problem areas.

Step 4: Propose a Solution

In cooperative learning groups:

1. Prepare a fact brochure that includes pictures and other documentation that you have collected.
2. Prepare a PowerPoint presentation that identifies the problem and proposes a solution.
3. Make the presentation to your classmates.

Sample Investigation: The Water Cycle

Created by Scott Easler, Middle School of Pacolet, Pacolet, SC

Overview:

Students are introduced to the water cycle and the amount and types of water on our planet. After basic information is covered, the students begin investigating the characteristics of water (pH, hardness, salinity, etc.).

Next the students practice using the LaMotte Water Testing Kits (chemical) in various applications. Students test the following types of water: tap water, bottled water, rainwater, creek water, pond water, and lake water.

The students finish up the unit by comparing pictures from the various water sources and look for differences.

Standards:

- Define groundwater, runoff, drainage divide, and drainage basin (watershed).
- Infer what happens to water that does not soak into the ground or evaporate.
- Analyze the factors that affect runoff.
- Differentiate between drainage divides and drainage basins using maps or aerial photography. Illustrate the relationships between groundwater and surface water in a watershed.
- Identify and illustrate groundwater zones including water table, zone of saturation, and zone of aeration.
- Identify technologies designed to reduce sources of point and non-point water pollution.

Digital Camera Use:

At each of the three outdoor locations (creek, pond, and lake) pictures are taken of the surrounding environments. These pictures are then arranged in a grid pattern at the end of the unit, and are accompanied by the test results obtained by the students. The students then compare the information from each of the three sites, and look for reasons as to why some tests are similar and some are different. Pollution effects can also be brought into this part of the unit and point and non-point sources of pollution are discussed.

Field Study:

At the last study site (lake), the students take a field study to the local water treatment facility and reservoir. After touring the plant the students take a pontoon ride on the lake where they conduct their water testing. They also have employees from the water company speak with them about career opportunities.

Sample Investigation: Buying a Car

Created by Mr. Marion D. Miller, Principal, Middle School of Pacolet, Pacolet, SC

Overview:

A car is probably the most common large item that consumers buy. This activity is designed to help students understand the questions they should ask before buying a car and help them determine the general price range for new and used cars.

Materials:

- internet connection
- digital cameras

Standards:

Consumer Economics

- The student will explain how consumers spend their budget to maximize the net benefits of their income.
- The student will identify present-day choices that have important future consequences.

Lesson:

Students will explore various sites on the Web that discuss buying a car. After visiting these sites, each student will write a step-by-step plan for buying a car that includes digital photography that illustrates what to look for and hazards to avoid when buying a car.

Guiding Questions:

1. How would you like to own a used car?
2. How would you like to own a new car?
3. Do you know what type of car you want?

Visit the following Web sites to gather information on buying a car.

Used Car Buying Tips: <http://www.usedcarbuyingtips.com/>
Buying a New Car: <http://www.bbb.org/library/newcar.asp>
New Car facts: <http://edmunds.com/edweb/manufact.html>
A Car Buying Guide: <http://www.smartsense.com/>
Used Car Facts: <http://edmunds.com/edweb/used/usedcars.html> Be sure to click on CONSUMER ADVICE to find extensive information.
Used Car Facts: <http://www.qtcu.asn.au/web.services/library/car.buying.html> This site provides information the consumer should consider when selecting a car. The list is very extensive. Make sure you view the entire page, there is some very important information on this page.

Sample Investigation: Buying a Car (continued)

After viewing the preceding sites and studying the information, the student should answer the following questions.

1. How do you get financing for your car?
2. Is it better to lease or own? Explain.
3. How would you know the value of your trade-in?
4. Write a step-by-step guide for buying a car. Write the guide as if you were teaching a class on buying a car.
5. Is it better to buy a used car or a new car?

Create a brochure that includes photographs that illustrate what to look for in a car and the hazards to avoid when purchasing your first vehicle.

Chapter 6

My Camera Is Full...What Next?

> *"The teacher is one who makes two ideas grow where only one grew before."*
>
> ***—Elbert Hubbard***

Putting Digital Images to Work

Up to this point, things have been going pretty smoothly. After developing some nifty lesson plans that incorporated this new world of digital photography, it seemed that the world was your oyster.

You can recall those first few tentative moments as students began clicking away as the electronic shutter made its distinctive clatter. Wow, it really was not a big deal at all. After instructing your students on the appropriate way to hold and shoot the camera and establishing some basic ground rules for what types of photos the students should avoid (i.e. Ms. Smith eating her lunch), the whole digital camera thing seemed downright easy.

Once the dust settled, it was time to get down to work and have students actually use all these great photos in amazing and engaging ways. There is one little issue though, especially if you are new to either computers or digital photography. Exactly how do I get all of these dozens, or even hundreds, of digital images from the camera to the computer? And then, of course, how do I arrange, edit, manipulate, export, and actually use these images in the framework of my lesson plan?

It is not as hard as it may appear. This chapter will demonstrate, in fairly general terms and examples, how to retrieve photos from a digital camera, manipulate them as necessary, and put them to use in projects and assignments.

Better Than Same-day Pickup

One of the greatest advantages of using digital photography is that images can be downloaded to a computer instantly. The days of waiting even an hour for a roll of film to be developed have passed. So, let's walk through a couple of different scenarios to show how to start putting your pictures to work.

Step 1: Moving Photos from the Camera to the Computer

As mentioned in Chapter 2, moving photos from the digital camera to the computer depends a lot on the type of digital camera you are using. This first example will illustrate how to download pictures stored on a digital camera that uses standard 3.5-inch floppy disks. In general, these are the steps to follow in order to download pictures from a 3.5-inch floppy disk.

1. Eject the floppy disk from the digital camera.
2. Insert the floppy disk into the A:Drive (floppy drive) on the computer.
3. Double-click the My Computer icon on the desktop.

Figure 6.1: My Computer

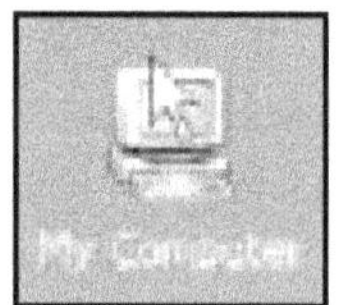

4. Double-click on the 3.5-inch floppy (A:) icon.
5. A listing of all files on the floppy disk will appear.

Figure 6.2: File List on Floppy Drive

SVI_0039.JPG	220 KB	JPEG Image
SVI_0040.JPG	230 KB	JPEG Image
SVI_0041.JPG	256 KB	JPEG Image
SVI_0042.JPG	290 KB	JPEG Image
SVI_0043.JPG	618 KB	JPEG Image
SVI_0044.JPG	274 KB	JPEG Image
SVI_0045.JPG	413 KB	JPEG Image
SVI_0046.JPG	290 KB	JPEG Image
SVI_0047.JPG	291 KB	JPEG Image
SVI_0048.JPG	244 KB	JPEG Image

6. Double-click on any file name. This will load the image in whatever program is set as the default viewer. (In English, this means that depending on the imaging software you are using and how your system is configured, an image file could open up in virtually any one of a number of programs. If you are using the Office Suite, for example, it will open in Photo Editor.) Not to worry though because these configurations are usually set without too much input required.
7. An alternative way to open a picture file from a 3.5-inch floppy disk is to open picture viewing/editing software and then open the file directly

within that program. This would be accomplished the same way as opening any other file in a Windows program. Simply go the File menu and click on Open. Navigate to the 3.5-inch floppy disk icon and double-click any files you wish to preview.

8. In order to clear the contents off of the floppy disk so it can be reused later on, it is often a good idea to save the images to the local hard drive (C: Drive).
9. After opening the file and deciding to keep it, follow these general steps to save the file to your hard drive.
10. Click on the File menu and choose Save As or in some cases Export (different software uses different commands).
11. Be sure to rename the file to something recognizable.
12. Be sure to save the file to a location (folder) that is easy to remember and easy to access (Tip—most computers come with a My Pictures folder already installed. It is not a bad place to store pictures while you are getting your feet wet.)

Figure 6.3: Save As Window

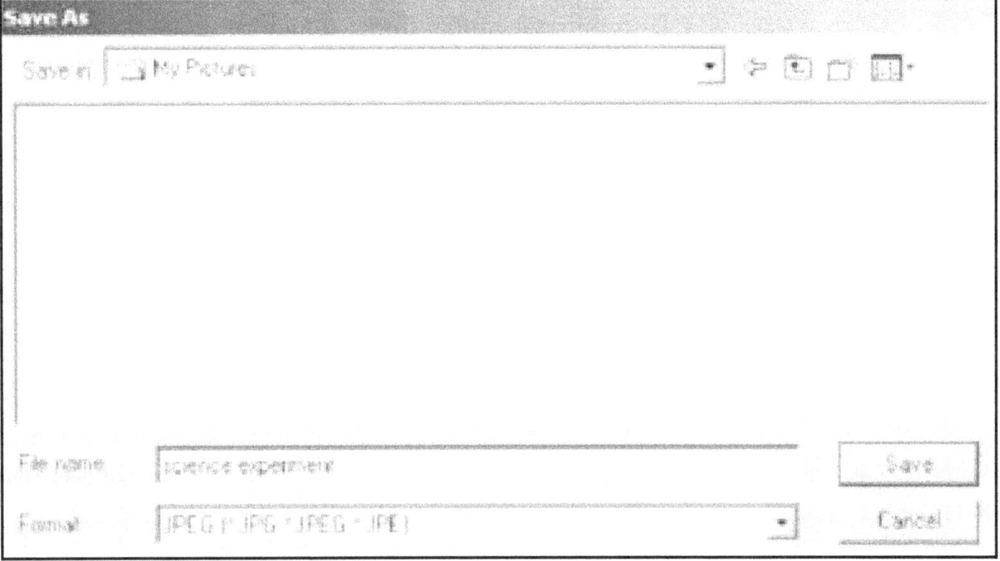

A Note on File Formats

It seems that for every way to take a picture there are even more file formats in which to save them. This should not be something with which to become preoccupied. For most lesson plan applications, just know that most common file formats (.bmp, .jpeg, .gif) will work fine. There are times when certain file formats are preferred because they make the file highly usable for specific purposes like Web page development, graphic design, or high-end publishing. For inclusion in day-to-day lesson plan activities, the three formats listed above should do the trick.

Opening Pictures When There Is No Floppy

The first part of Step 1 described how to transfer a digital picture when it has been saved on a floppy disk. As you know from Chapter 2, many cameras, especially newer ones, use alternate storage methods such as flash memory cards. This means that files are downloaded to a computer in an alternative manner, usually through a USB cable connection. This sounds difficult, but really all it means is that you attach a special cable that most likely came with the camera to a special port on the computer. As you have probably already guessed, this port is called a USB port. Again, keep in mind that there are many variations on this process. What follows is a very general description of transferring picture files from a camera to a computer via a USB cable.

1. Install any special software that may have come with the digital camera.
2. Attach the USB cable to an empty USB port on the computer.
3. Attach the other end of the USB cable to the appropriate port on the camera.
4. Power on the camera.
5. In some cases, after double clicking on the My Computer icon, the digital camera will appear listed along with the hard drive, floppy drive, and CD-ROM drive. Other times, it may be necessary to run the software that came with the camera to download the pictures.

Figure 6.4: My Camera Icon

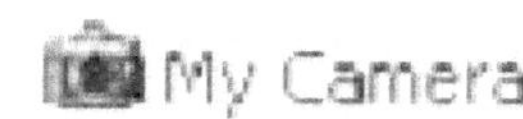

System Folder

6. If the digital camera is accessible through My Computer, then simply open, view, and save the pictures in the same manner as you would with a floppy disk.
7. If special software that came with the camera is being used, simply follow the manufacturer's instructions on downloading the digital camera pictures to your computer.

Step 2: Making Changes
It Looks Different Than I Thought It Would

Even if you read the manual that came with your digital camera or received special training, there will be those times when the picture opens and … it is flipped the wrong way, or is too bright, or just needs some touching up. Most common photo editing software can fix all of these things and then some. Because of the sheer number of different photo editing programs and even the number of differences between a newer and older version of the same software, the following demonstrations will be extremely general.

Getting It Straight

Inevitably, you or your students will take a picture and realize when you view it that it is upside down or sideways. This should not arouse panic. It simply means that the picture will need to be rotated to be viewed right-side up.

Figure 6.5: The Wrong Way

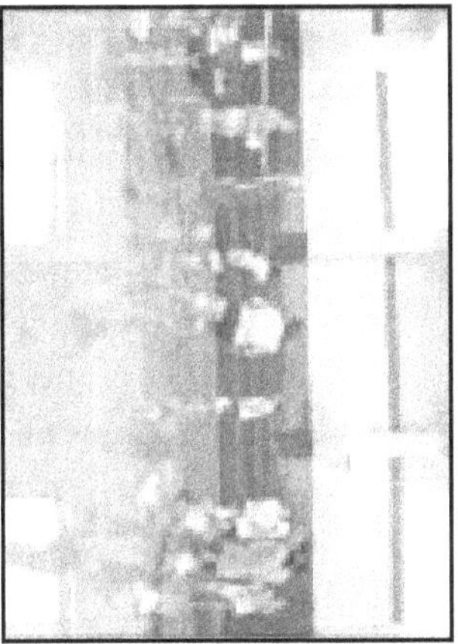

Here we have a perfectly good picture of volleyball practice, but the imaged is flipped 90 degrees. Most photo editing programs have a menu item called Rotate Image or Rotate Picture. Select the appropriate option and rotate the picture as necessary. In this example, the picture would need to be rotated 90 degree CCW (counterclockwise).

Figure 6.6: The Right Direction

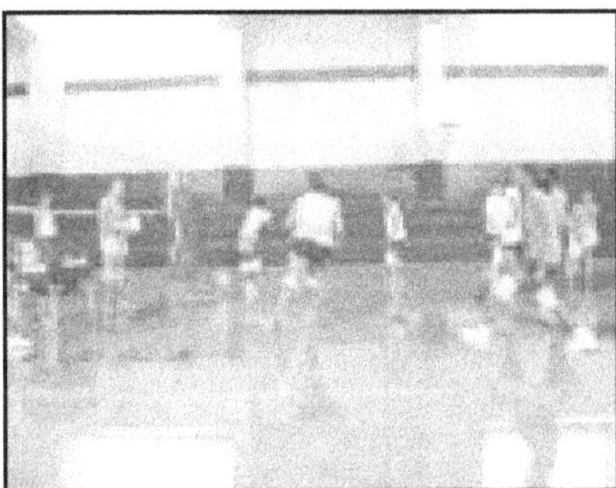

Resizing Pictures

A common surprise digital camera users experience is that when they view pictures on the computer... they look awfully BIG. Most cameras shoot pictures at or above your computer's screen resolution. That means if your computer's display is at 640 × 480, and the camera is taking pictures at 1024 × 768, the picture will appear much larger and will not fit entirely on the screen. When resizing pictures, keep in mind that the size of the picture on the screen does not mean the picture will print at that size. When looking at the properties of an image, most photo editing programs indicate the pixel size (on the screen) and the print size in inches or centimeters. In either case, resizing a picture usually means finding a menu called something like Image and then selecting Image Size. Change the image size settings to whatever value you need.

Cropping—It's Not Just for Farmers

As you look at digital pictures, it will soon become clear that they could be improved if unnecessary scenery could be removed. Cropping is simply cutting away parts of a digital photo that are extraneous to the subject of the picture. Notice in the following picture, the wall above the students and the floor draw away from the focus of the picture.

Figure 6.7: Needs Cropping

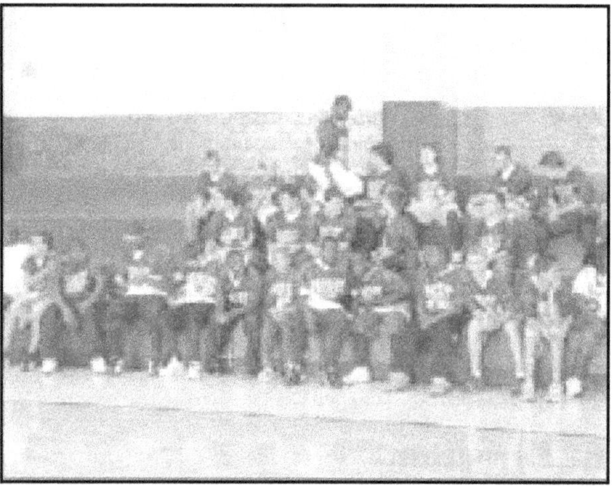

Fortunately, most photo editing software offers the cropping option. In general, to crop a picture simply select the part of an image that you want to stay (this would be done by clicking and dragging the mouse pointer over the desired area). Then, simply click on the Crop menu located somewhere within the photo editing software. The end result is a picture with a stronger focus on what is important … students.

Figure 6.8: Cropped Picture

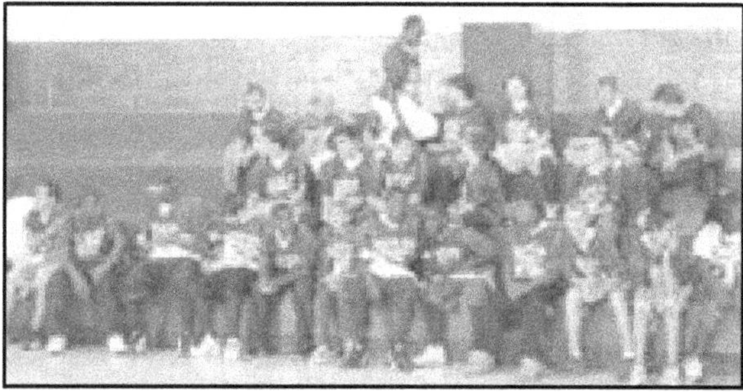

A Picture is Worth a Thousand Words, but the Words Don't Hurt Either

Depending on the final use of a picture, it is often appropriate to add text directly onto a picture. Most photo editing software contains a text tool that allows you to add text to a picture.

Figure 6.9: Watching the Game

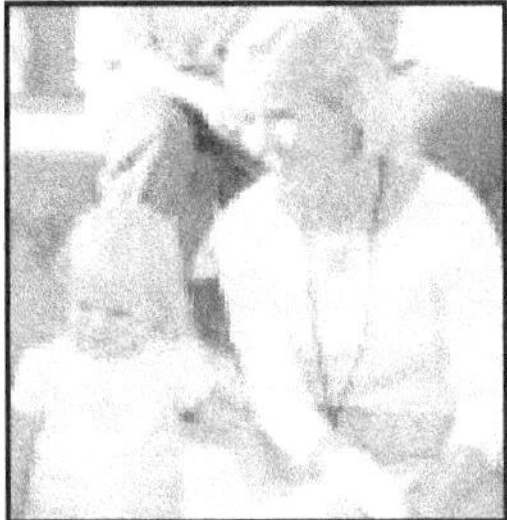

Now, here is the same picture with some text.

Figure 6.10: Text on Photo

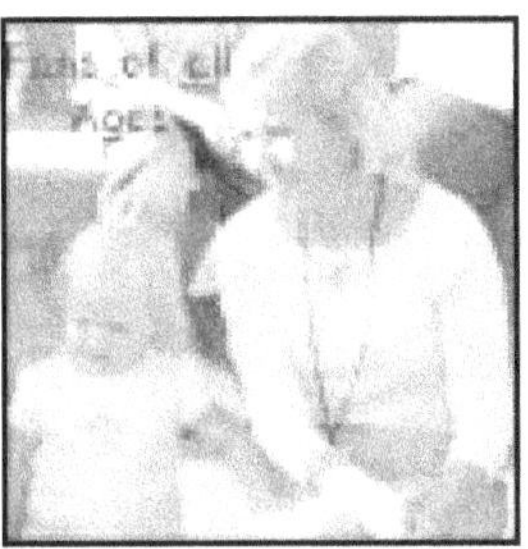

Step 3: Putting Pictures to Use

This chapter has been mostly concerned with demonstrating how to download pictures from a digital camera to a computer as well as how do perform some basic image manipulation to enhance your pictures. Keep in mind that the main goal is learning to use the pictures once they are the way you want them. There are countless ways to incorporate digital photos into a variety of software programs you may be using to teach lessons. Here are some general suggestions for places to use your digital photos.

- Word processing documents such as book reports, research papers, and creating writing assignments.
- Slideshow presentations that describe a process, provide a virtual tour, or illustrate a historical timeline.
- Graphic organizers or thinking map software.
- Student or teacher Web pages.

Chapter 7

Using Your Digital Images

"The principal goal of education is to create men who are capable of doing new things, not simply of repeating what other generations have done—men who are creative, inventive, and discoverers."
—Jean Piaget

Making It Happen

One exciting aspect of incorporating digital photos into your lesson plans is the ability of students to use them in ways we never imagined. The ability of digital photography to unleash creativity and inventiveness in students is truly amazing. While some teachers are satisfied using the digital camera to shoot photos only to later print them out to pin-up or use in projects, many others are incorporating digital photos into a variety of other technological applications that add excitement and vigor to the classroom. This chapter provides general examples of using digital photos with widely used software that is found in many schools. The first section covers digital photo usage in MS PowerPoint to create engaging lesson plans and for student presentations. Next, we will look at incorporating digital photos while using Inspiration, a wonderful thinking map software application. Web pages for schools, teachers, and students have become nearly universal. This section covers using digital photos in some common Web authoring software packages and some special considerations. To round things out, we will show how digital photos can be used in word processing activities with MS Word.

Making Your Point

PowerPoint is an ideal way to begin using digital photos quickly and fairly easily with students. PowerPoint is a slideshow program that is designed specifically to present material in a visually eye-catching manner. Because of the added ability to quickly add animation, music, and sound effects, PowerPoint can be a very stimulating instructional tool. The next few steps will cover inserting a digital picture into a PowerPoint slideshow and some things that can be done once the picture is there.

Inserting a Picture into a PowerPoint Slideshow

This tutorial begins assuming that the reader possesses some experience using PowerPoint, such as opening a new slideshow.

1. Create a new PowerPoint slideshow or open an existing slideshow.
2. Choose a slide format. If the digital picture is a large one, try inserting a blank slide. PowerPoint also offers several slide templates that reserve space specifically for a picture. Choose the one that suits your needs.

Figure 7.1: Inserting a New Slide

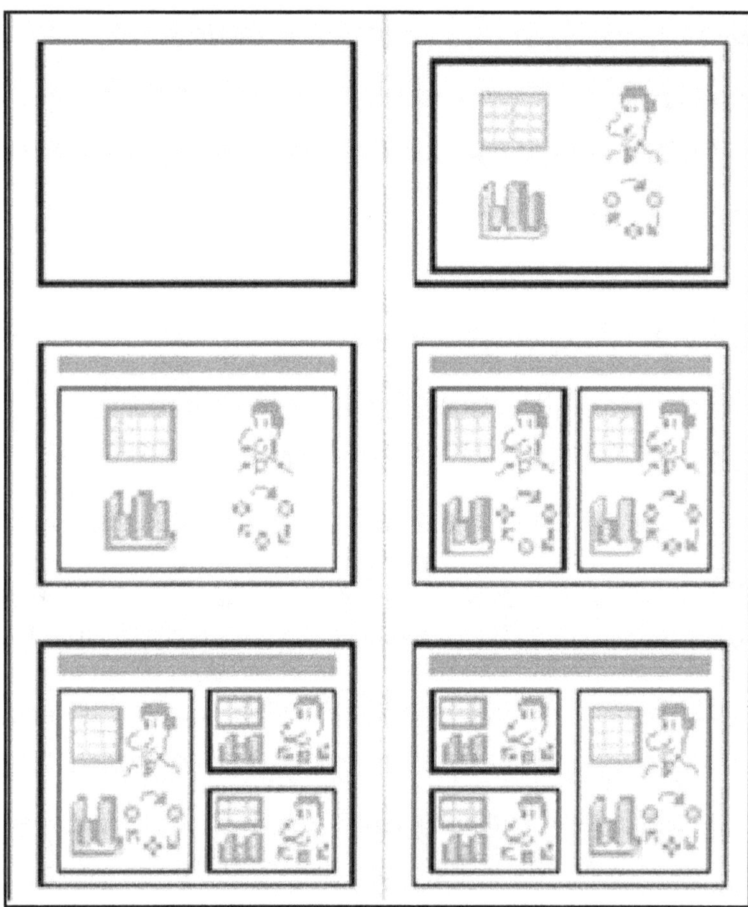

3. After selecting the appropriate slide, you are now ready to insert a digital photo.
4. Click one time on the Insert menu, move your cursor to Picture, and then select From File from the sub-menu.

Figure 7.2: Inserting an Image

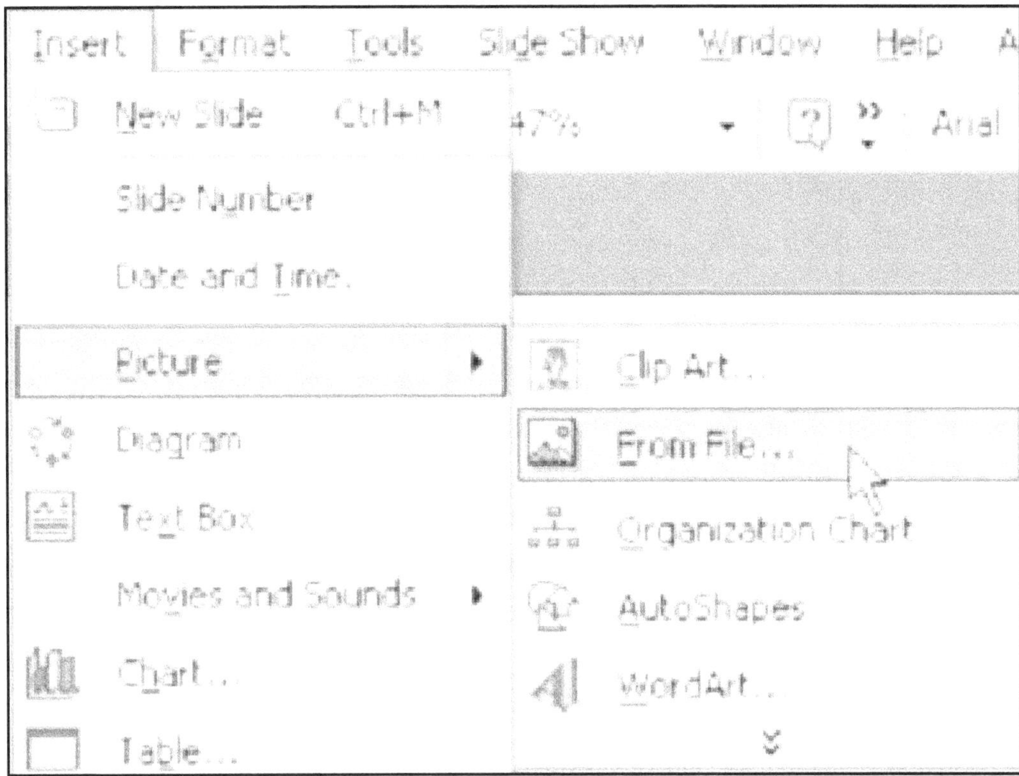

5. Navigate to the folder location of your pictures. When you locate the picture, click on it one time and click on the Insert button.

Figure 7.3: Inserting a Picture from Your Picture Folder

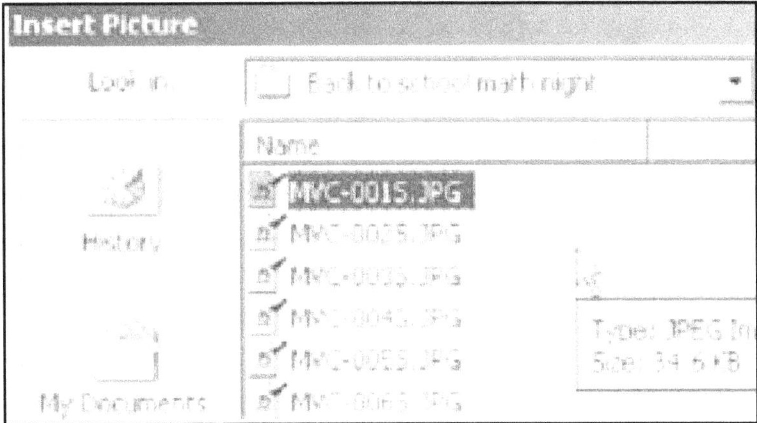

6. The picture will now appear in the slide ready to receive any special effects.

Figure 7.4: Slide With Picture

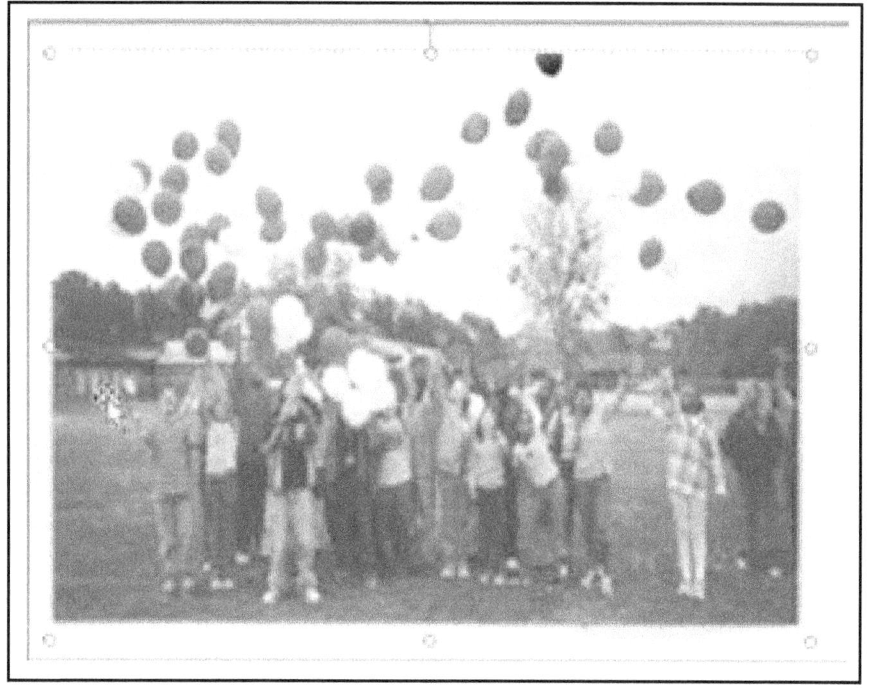

Get Inspired

Inspiration is a powerful way for students to use digital photos to enhance their learning. As with PowerPoint, it is fairly easy to insert pictures into an Inspiration diagram.

1. Create a new Inspiration diagram or open an existing one.
2. Click on an area of the screen where you wish to place the picture.
3. Click one time on the Edit menu and click on Insert Graphic

Figure 7.5: Inserting a Graphic in an Inspiration Diagram

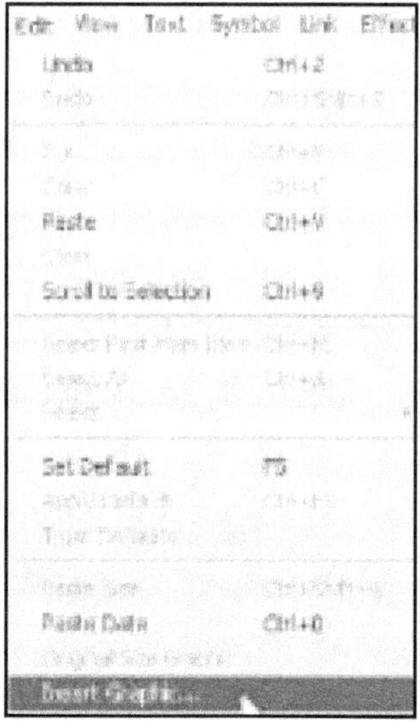

4. Navigate to the appropriate folder where your pictures are stored and double-click on the picture you wish to insert.
5. Once pictures have been inserted, use Inspiration to label information, make connections, and describe processes.

Figure 7.6: The Scientific Process

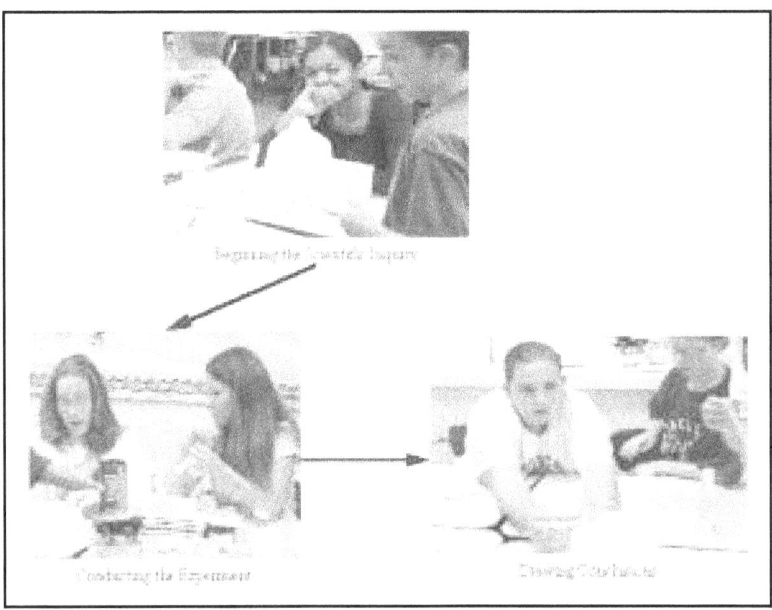

Getting Ready for the Web

One of the great uses of the Web is the ability to share not only text but also informative, stimulating visual content. The large number of Web authoring software programs prevents any kind of detailed demonstration. For this example, we will use Netscape 7.0 that is a free download and comes with a more than adequate authoring tool called Netscape Composer.

1. To access Netscape Composer, launch the Netscape program by double clicking on its icon.
2. When Netscape loads, it will be in the Web browser view called Navigator.
3. To switch to Composer, click one time on the Window menu and select Composer.

Figure 7.7: Switch to Netscape Composer

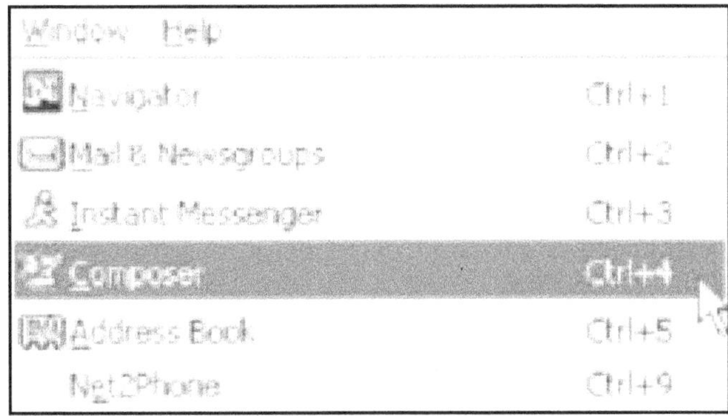

4. From the Composer window, either begin working on a brand new Web page or open an existing Web page.
5. To insert a saved digital photo, either click one time on the Insert menu and select Image or click one time on the Image icon on the toolbar.

Figure 7.8: Inserting an Image from a Menu

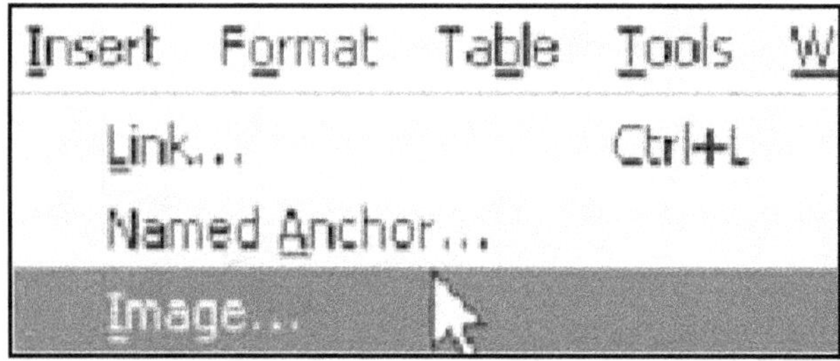

Figure 7.9: Inserting an Image Using the Image Icon

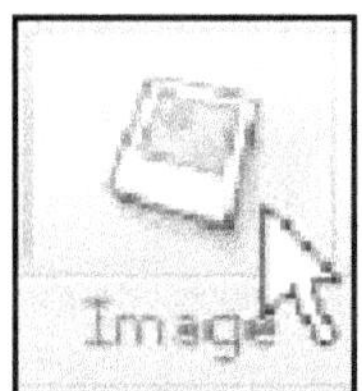

6. A dialogue window will open asking you to browse for the location of the picture file. Click one time on the Choose File button to browse for the photo. One bonus of using Netscape Composer is that it will generate an image preview that also includes the dimensions of the photo about to be inserted. Click OK.

Figure 7.10: Choosing a File to Insert

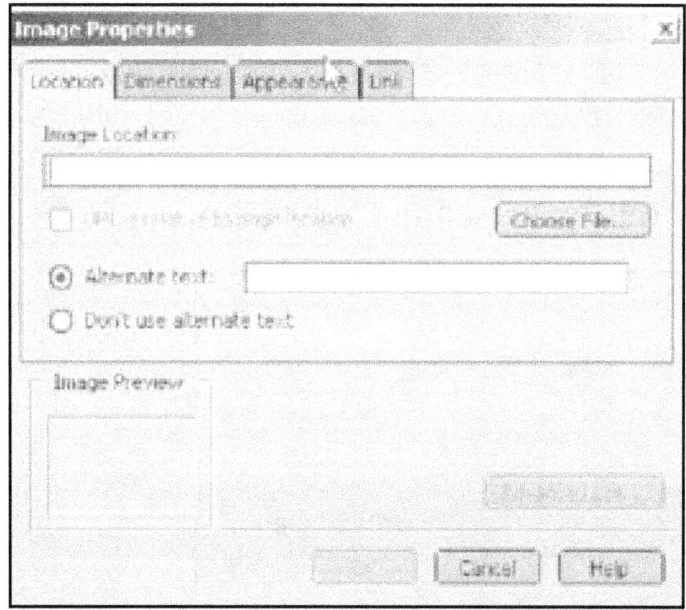

Figure 7.11: Previewing the Image

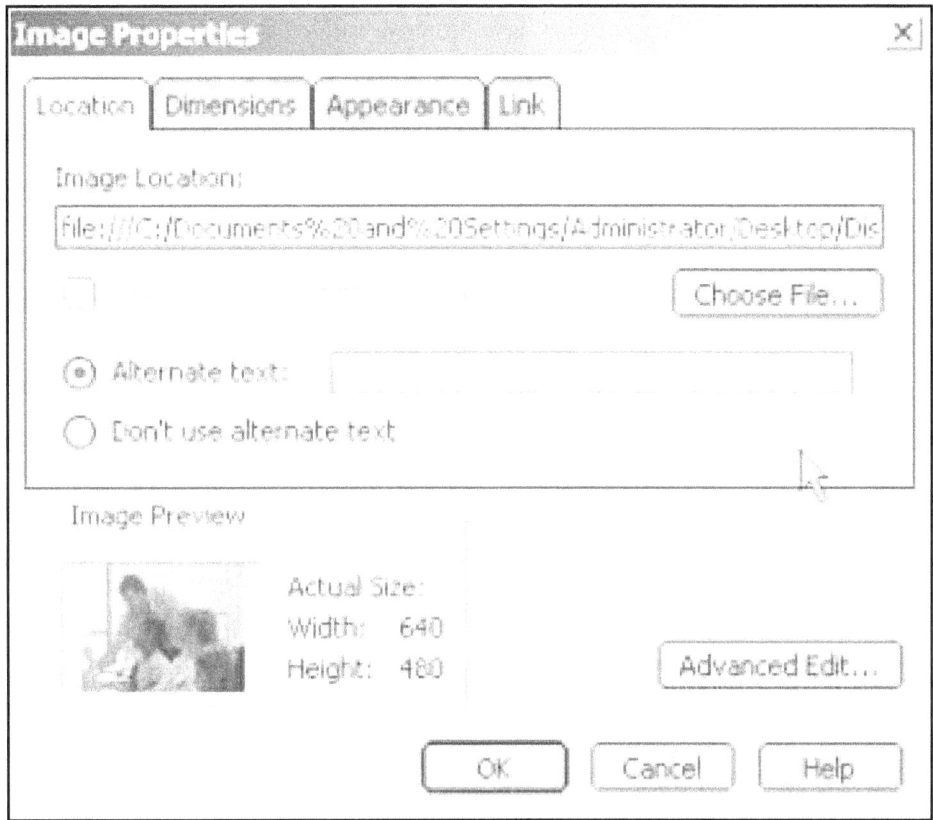

Figure 7.12: Inserted Image

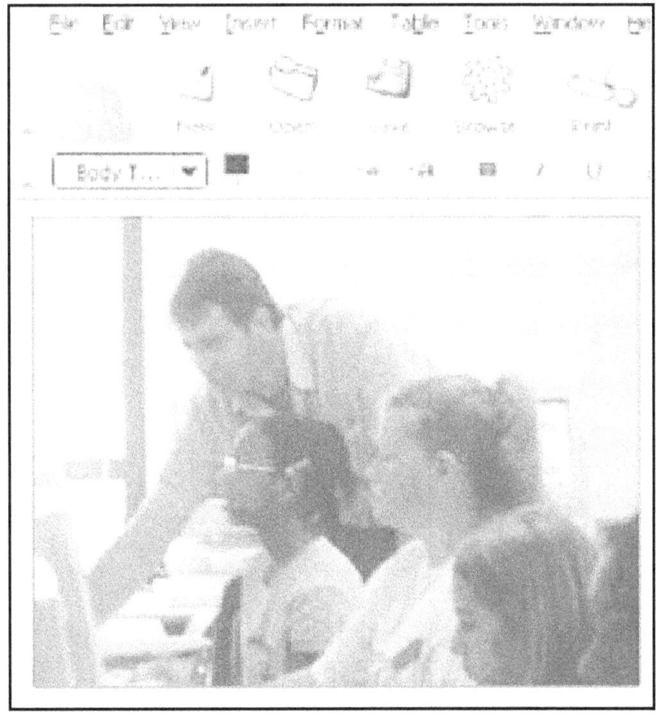

Word is for More than Words

If you are reading this page, you have already realized that Word is useful for more than just typing. Like PowerPoint, inserting a digital photo into a Word document is a breeze. The steps are the same.

1. Begin a new Word document or open an existing one.
2. Click the mouse pointer on the screen location where you want the picture to be inserted. The cursor will flash at the insertion point.
3. Click one time on the Insert menu, select Picture, and then From File from the sub-menu.
4. Navigate to the folder location of your pictures. When you locate the picture, click on it one time and click on the Insert button.
5. The picture is now inserted in your Word document.

In a Hurry

Of course there will be those times when you just want a quick and easy way to display digital photos to a class for immediate discussion or analysis. In this case, a slideshow viewer is a good option. Slideshow viewers are typically very small software programs whose main purpose is to just rotate through a collection of images that you designate. To find one that is right for you, navigate on the Internet to Download.com <http://www.download.com> and type in a search using the keyword "slideshow." While some are free to try for a certain time frame, others are completely free and totally functional. The following example demonstrates the use of a simple program called Slideshow 1.20. All that is required is that you browse to the location of a folder containing digital pictures in JPEG format. The other settings are self-explanatory. When everything is set up how you want it, simply click on the Start Slideshow Now button and watch all the images rotate through on your screen.

Figure 7.13: Slideshow 1.20

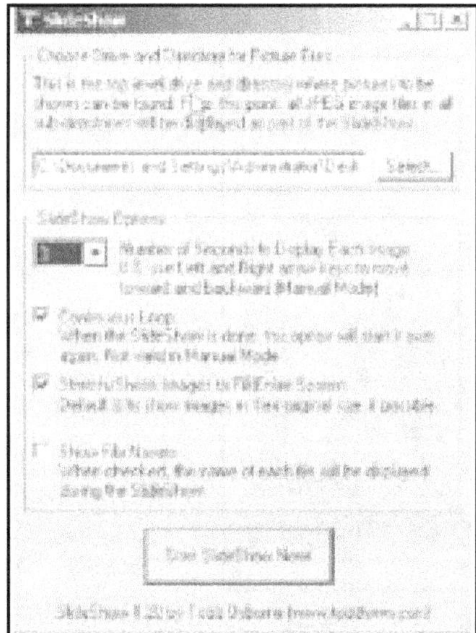

Chapter 8

Finding Support

> *"It's not the hours you put in your work that counts; it's the work you put in the hours."*
>
> ***—Sam Ewing***

While we would all agree that visual aids and hands-on activities are two of the most effective ways to deliver content, it is often time consuming to come up with fresh ideas.

Ideas for projects in all subject areas are readily available on the Web. English and social studies provide a natural link for using digital imagery. Projects such as *Through the Eyes of a Child*, <http://www.eyesofachild.com/> encourage students to explore the world through photography. In this particular project, professional photographers are matched with children as mentors.

Another engaging project reported in *Wired New*, <http://www.wired.com/news/school/0,1383,53134,00.html?tw=wn_ascii> is *Building the City—Digitally*. This project provides children an opportunity to recreate their own city through a database of digital imagery.

Digital imagery can also be used with mathematics. With the emphasis on counting, sorting, and comparing sets of objects common in mathematics, it is easy to see how digital imagery can be used effectively. For the youngest to the most sophisticated learner, recognizing and describing simple patterns, shapes, and sizes of figures and objects folds naturally into digital images. Students can be actively engaged through the use of manipulatives and digital imagery. How better to look for patterns and relationships than exploring the real world with a digital camera?

Resources that rely on digital imagery for mathematics can be found throughout the Web. One of the best sites, however, is *The National Math Trail*, <http://www.nationalmathtrail.org/>. The emphasis of *The National Math Trail* is on discovering and sharing math objects in the student's own world. Using a variety of sources ranging from video to photos, students create math problems that relate to what they see. In one example, a student explores Stone Mountain (Georgia) and relates digital images to mathematics. The site also indexes the submitted information according to grade level and math topic.

Figure 8.1: The National Math Trail

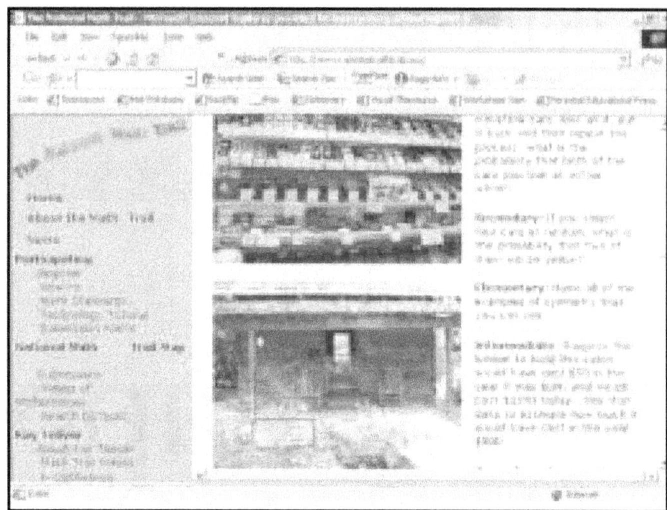

This is a wonderful opportunity to bring the excitement of real-world math into the classroom. It can be adapted to any mathematics topic of the K–12 curriculum. By following the "Technology Tutorial" link from the navigation menu, students and teachers can view simple ways to utilize technology in preparing entries—including a template for the creation of Web page submissions. There is also an online, self-teaching guide on digital communication.

Science is another core subject that places emphasis on using the senses to gather information. Students are expected to develop skills in posing simple questions, measuring, sorting, classifying, and communicating information about the natural world. From Harvard's ENT Gallery, there are sample lessons on many topics including a very well developed project called *Water Habitat. Harvard's ENT Gallery: The Water Habit Project* is available at <http://learnweb.harvard.edu/ent/gallery/pop3/pop3_1.cfm>.

Figure 8.2: The Water Habitat

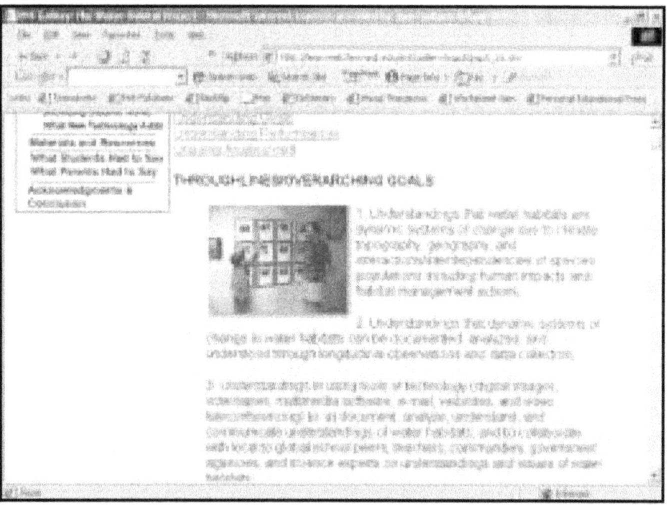

Other Resources

Teachers and media specialists are creative people. Some sites that offer wonderful ideas for using digital cameras have been created by the teachers and students who use them. Explore the following:

75 Ways to Use Your Digital Camera,
<http://www.semo.net/suburb/mgilmer/digcam/index.htm>
Classroom Applications for the Digital Camera,
<http://nt.etc.davis.k12.ut.us/curriculum/lessons/camera2.pdf>
Digital Camera Poetry Books,
<http://www.kent.k12.wa.us/curriculum/tech/lessons/5/dig_cam_poetry.htm>
The Digital Camera and Its Uses in Your Classroom, compiled by Andy Ventress, Casio Incorporated,
<http://tli.jefferson.k12.ky.us/stlp/Virtual%20notebook/78Casio%20emh.PDF>.
Connecting Teachers & Students Tutorials,
<http://www.paducah.k12.ky.us/curriculum/online_tutorials.htm>
Using a Digital Camera in the Classroom,
<http://www.msdlt.k12.in.us/msdlt/StaffDevelopment/digitalcameras.htm>
K–12 Ideas for Using the Digital Camera,
<http://avia-hs.odedodea.edu/et/ET-TIPS/DIGCAM.html>
Using a Digital Camera in the Classroom,
<http://www.richardson.k12.tx.us/schools/lhe/lhecamera.htm>
Classroom Applications for the Digital Camera (contains a list of 52 ideas for using digital pictures),
<http://k-12.pisd.edu/techs/dhitt/digital/camideas.htm>.
Kodak: K–12 Lesson Plans,
<http://www.kodak.com/US/en/digital/dlc/plus/chapter5/lessonPlans.shtml>
The Digital Camera in Education,
<http://www.drscavanaugh.org/digitalcamera/>
Digital Cameras in the Classroom,
<http://members.ozemail.com.au/~cumulus/digcam.htm>
Teacher to Teacher,
<http://www.brunswick.k12.me.us/lon/lonlinks/digicam/teacher/home.html>
Casio Classroom: 1001 Uses for a Digital Camera,
<http://pegasus.cc.ucf.edu/~ucfcasio/qvuses.htm>
Going Digital in the Classroom,
<http://www.forsyth.k12.ga.us/sbeck/digital/goingdigital.htm>
Using the Digital Camera in the Primary Classroom,
<http://www.hardin.k12.ky.us/res_techn/TEC/digitalcamera/primary.htm>
Digitizing the Primary Classroom,
<http://www.techlearning.com/db_area/archives/WCE/archives/heese6.htm>
Using Digital Cameras for Classroom Projects, (offers suggestions for projects using digital cameras),
<http://www.4teachers.org/techalong/anderson/index.shtml>.

Practical Uses for the Digital Camera,
<http://www.4teachers.org/techalong/anderson/cahand.html>

Digital Photography Resources,
<http://www.clifton.k12.nj.us/mediacenter/digitalphoto.html>

Fujifilm PhotoPals—Curriculum Connections,
<http://www.fujifilmphotopals.com/teachers/archives/compare.asp>

Kathy Schrock's Guide for Educators—Digital Gadgets for the Classroom,
<http://school.discovery.com/schrockguide/gadgets.html>

Index

About the Authors

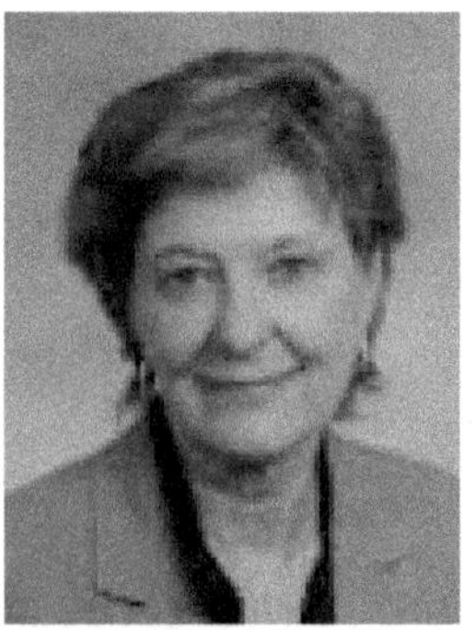

Mary Ploski Seamon is a native of Connecticut and now resides in South Carolina. She is the mother of two children—Trevor of Los Angeles, California and Socrates of San Jose, California. Mary is a former English teacher, assistant principal, and principal at D. W. Daniel High School in Clemson, South Carolina. She credits Dr. Jim Ray, superintendent of Spartanburg School District 3, for creating the vision of technology integration.

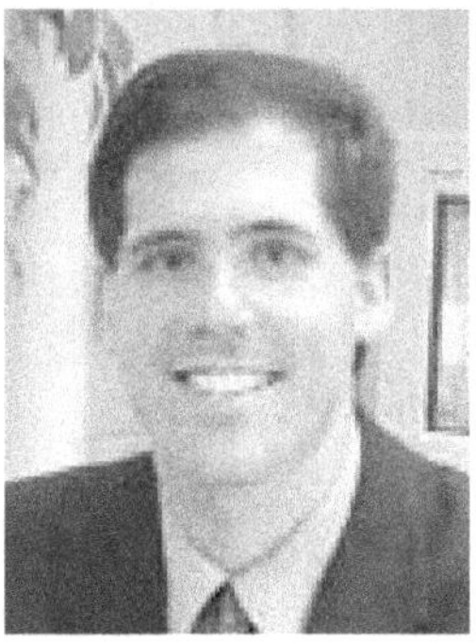

Eric J. Levitt is a native of Long Island. Eric and his wife, Carmen, make their home in South Carolina. Eric taught high school social studies in Grapevine, Texas. For the past three years, he has been the technology trainer for Spartanburg School District 3 in South Carolina.

www.ingramcontent.com/pod-product-compliance
Lightning Source LLC
LaVergne TN
LVHW061253100826
845148LV00008B/1118
* 9 7 8 1 5 8 6 8 3 0 9 5 3 *